COME, LET US PLAY!

By the same author

AT EASE WITH STRESS

PEOPLE NEED STILLNESS

CHRIST, STRESS AND GLORY

GIFTS FROM HILDEGARD

HEALTH AT SCHOOL

LIVING WITH GOD AT THE VICARAGE

TURNING THE DOWNSIDE UP

'The Dancing Madonna' by Maureen Coatman
Church of St Luke, Duston, Northampton.

COME, LET US PLAY!

PLAYFULNESS AND PRAYER

Wanda Nash

Illustrations by
Sister Mary Stephen Grindon-Welch CRSS

First published in 1999 by
Darton, Longman and Todd Ltd
1 Spencer Court
140–142 Wandsworth High Street
London SW18 4JJ

ISBN 0-232-52345-2

A catalogue record for this book is available from the British Library.

Several versions of the Bible have been quoted in this book. They have been identified by the following initials:

AV	–	Authorised Version
REB	–	Revised English Bible
JB	–	Jerusalem Bible
NJB	–	New Jerusalem Bible
NRSV	–	New Revised Standard Version
GNB	–	Good News Bible
The Message	–	see Booklist

Designed by Sandie Boccacci
Phototypeset in $8\frac{1}{2}/13\frac{3}{4}$pt Leawood Book by Intype London Ltd
Printed and bound in Great Britain by Page Bros, Norwich, Norfolk

To Trevor, my helpmeet and playmate, both.

God is gone up with a merry noise.

Psalm 47:5

'I, God, am your playmate!
I will lead the child in you in wonderful ways
for I have chosen you.'

Mechthilde of Magdeburg[1]

Our heart is wide open to you. In return –
I speak as to children – open wide your hearts also.

2 Corinthians 6:12–13 NRSV

CONTENTS

ACKNOWLEDGEMENTS

I wish to acknowledge, primarily, the inadequacy of the pronouns 'he', 'him' and 'his' in reference to God. The mystery of the inclusive gender of God, together with the beyond-gender of God, cannot be confined within a single range of personal pronoun. To do so is a sad compromise, but it has to be so for practicality. I am sure God laughs alongside our clumsiness, and forgives; I hope you will too.

I want to thank the many people who, out of their great generosity, have agreed to let me use their material. Whether it is personal experience that I have been lucky enough to share with them, or written words that have moved me, this book would have been poor without them. I am deeply indebted to them all.

Specific thanks are due to those who have given permission for their copyright to be used: in alphabetical order they are: Les Acklam, priest, for the description of his experience of laughter in prayer; Father Byrne for an extract from *The Laughter of Christ*; Helen Caswell for the extract from her book *God Must Like to Laugh*; Anne Lewin, for permission to use her poem, 'Jeu d'Esprit'; Curtis Brown for 'Prayer of the Goat' by Carmen Bernos de Gasztold; Marion McCall for her poems from *Dreaming in Willochra*. The books in which the above feature are detailed in the Booklist on p. 118, as are the sources of all quotations in the present book.

Visually, this book is held high by Sister Mary Stephen's illustrations, and I want to thank her again for her commitment and compliance – a rare duo! Maureen Coatman and the Church of St

Luke, Duston, have enriched the book with the photo of their *Dancing Madonna*; and thanks are also due to MMP Cambridge for the photograph of Matthew on p. 96.

I am deeply grateful to Bishop Simon Barrington-Ward for his Foreword.

This book would not have reached the public had it not been for the patience and creativity of the team at DLT. My thanks to them are uppermost in both my heart and mind.

And last but by no means least, I thank my four daughters, who taught me how to play.

WANDA NASH

FOREWORD

One evening at dusk in Howrah railway station in Calcutta, during a lull between trains, a yell of excitement came from a little family group of the poorest of the poor, sitting on the platform. A kindly food-seller packing up for the night had handed a hunk of bread to the youngest of them, a small boy, and it was he who had yelled as he grasped the bread and began to dance. And as he danced everyone clapped in time and someone started to sing. The boy pirouetted to and fro in ecstasy holding up the bread like an offering as though the joy would never end. There are encounters like this which stay with you and somehow in an instant lift you out of all your preoccupations and disclose to you what life is really about.

This book of Wanda Nash's is just such an encounter. Through it I have seen afresh that playing and praying are both alike ways of entry into the movement towards that final wholeness our world so desperately needs. They belong together. Praying is not so much trying to get through on a faulty line as plunging into a hidden river. As we let it carry us, we find it is flowing from its source in the divine love towards the ocean of God's ultimate goal. And true playing equally frees us from the rigid self-concern of so much religion and worldliness alike as we reach out to grasp and be grasped by that 'Kingdom of right relationships'. I remember a wonderful host in Nigeria who drew all his guests, young and old alike into laughter and friendship as we were caught up into an absurd game called 'I have a Hippopotamus . . .!' That scene lives on and has inspired all his guests in our varied struggles towards true humanity.

Wanda leads us through a marvellous sequence of rediscoveries of the child in us, of the sheer free playfulness of grace, in the Bible, in Jesus himself, in God and the whole creation, in the therapeutic potential of real 'belly laughter' flowing out of the healing acceptance of our own absurdity and the release of our real selves, and in the genuine merriment of the mystics. Her rich assembly of quotations and illustrations we can dwell in and keep drawing upon. But her central insight is that of the Clown, the Holy Fool, the seemingly 'handicapped', the suffering and even, most movingly, children in pain, where the cross and the resurrection are fused in one, the glory of God in the broken Christ is fully realised. There the terrible darkness of the tragedy of this world fails in the end to extinguish the Light. In this Divine Comedy, as it will be at the last, play and delight have the final word.

So, as we step through the gate of the year into the new Millennium there is much in this lovely book that gives us reason to hold it in our hands. It looks as if we have hardly begun to live in the way we were made for, the way we have been given in Christ, of that love which casts out fear. Here we are shown that in the great upheaval of values and the melting pot of faiths and ideologies which the new Millennium seems to hold in store, there is no need to cling to past defences. We must learn to go out with a trust that leads into prayerfulness and playfulness, like the Israelites coming out of Egypt, 'our mouth filled with laughter and our tongue with joy' or like all the peoples of the earth coming up towards the final feast on Mount Zion, to the city through which the river flows, where the Cross has put on leaves and become the Tree of Life for the healing of the nations. 'And a little child shall lead them.' It could be that child on the platform at Howrah station – a glimpse of the Christ child?

+ SIMON BARRINGTON-WARD

INTRODUCTION

Our image of God is so Solemn. For centuries the 'approved' approach to God has been one of solemnity, seriousness, and staid gravity. Reverence is right. This book is about an Unsolemn approach to an Unsolemn God.

Most of life may be serious; some of it is downright dreary. Tragedy and despair, boredom and tediousness, hopelessness and copelessness are easy to find in our lives today. It's easy to awfulize the situations facing us in our modern world. Even children have to be taught to be suspicious and distrust strangeness. And yet, if I found that my children approached me always solemn, always polite, contrite, and on their good behaviour, I would soon realise there was a gaping hole in our relationship. A yawning gap where there should be confidence and intimacy. Their guardedness in my company would squeal of inhibition and constraint, not of love. So when I, child of God, never let up on the solemnity of my approach to my divine Father, how does he feel about it? When I constantly tell him how sorry I am, hanging my head so I don't meet his gaze, and speak only of all the terribleness of his world, does that please him? Would he want more of the same? Awe and wonder are clothed in many different ways.

The blueprint of creation as it is given to us by God contains stark contrasts of work and play, death and life, sorrow and joy, each one growing from the other and each one enlightening the other. There are times and spaces for all the range of the emotions that God has designed for us. Some of them we neglect more than others. For instance, although Jesus was emphatic about wanting to hand it to us, **restfulness** has often been ignored, although nowadays more people are relearning its value through the leading of the Holy Spirit. **Humour** is another we neglect, or misunderstand; perhaps it is more difficult. **Childlikeness**, which implies a certain letting go, and a mutuality of delight, is a subject of which we hear very little. That is where this book comes in.

The book will build on a platform of writings from people who have been prominent in the twentieth century – from Dorothy Sayers to Roly Bain – and it will make use of bricks taken from the Scriptures and some of the best-loved mystics. These various quotations will be grouped around four things:

- The book is about playing, not erudition, though I hope many readers will find new food for thought. Its subject, though playful, is about the profound relationship between humans and God.
- It is a book about joking, though not about jokes. With our inbuilt and deeply conditioned resistance we find it hard to think of God joking with us and with creation. Yet joking with the family, laughing uproariously together, is a prime delight for all of us. Not laughing at anyone or anything, but just because we all feel good about being together. Our insistence upon being serious with God heavily limits our experience of the Godhead. Although it takes a sort of abandoned trust that is politically incorrect, we deprive ourselves of a certain fire-in-the-belly if it gets neglected. That astonishing spark of connectedness that suddenly makes sense of things.
- The book concerns prayer, but you won't find a large collection of prayers. In prayer, we put into words our deepest hopes and longings; too easily and too often we project the things we most want onto God in the form of imperatives. Just take a quick look

at some of our most commonly used prayers: Help me! Protect me! Save me! Heal him/her! Forgive me! Grant her/him! Make them! If a guest in my house chose to speak to me in those terms, I wouldn't know which way to turn. Jesus, himself, was a guest who was enormously popular, and as such he used words to reach people, not to put them off. Now, in heaven, he is my Host: one who welcomes me daily, hourly, minute-by-minute into his presence.

- Perhaps the content of this book concerns the 'anima' more than the 'animus' of our relationship with God. It is about releasing more of the anima into the spirituality of both men and women, and loosening up some of the constraining animus. The difference between the two has been largely unrecognised or suppressed for the last twelve centuries, and it is the animus that has dominated the prayer life of both women and men in that time. This book is about opening up to the width of the range of ways to reach towards the Triune Godhead. Highlighting the anima is an enrichment more than a corrective, and it is a task for all of us, men and women alike. As Pia Buxton said in an address to the Franciscans in 1987:

> . . . the feminine concept of community is a circle, while the male effort works with a pyramid. Prayer is ultimately for our wholeness, ultimately we must try and receive the gift with the whole of ourselves; it will make us more alive, more vulnerable: it will highlight our darkness and our lightness. Prayer is not for personal peace but for the kingdom.

Playfulness, trust, abandonment, delight, gaiety and laughter are well represented in much of the writing which describes our early stretchings in spirituality. Take the following, for example:

I keep Yahweh before me always . . .
So my heart rejoices, my soul delights,
my body too will rest secure . . .
You will teach me the path of life,
unbounded joy in your presence,
at your right hand, delight for ever.

(Psalm 16:8,9,11 NJB)

And:

. . . The children of Zion delight in their king;
they shall dance in praise of his name,
play to him on tambourines and harp!
. . . The faithful exult in glory,
shout for joy as they worship him,
praising God to the heights with their voices . . .

(Psalm 148:2–3,5 NJB)

How much more playful can you get, than

You will go out with joy
  and be led forth in peace;
before you the mountains and hills will break into cries
  of joy
and all the trees of the countryside will clap their hands.

(Isaiah 55:12 REB)

The strangest thing is that the passion of Jesus Christ becomes all the more significant and real, actual and terrible having entered into the playfulness which Jesus so enjoyed. It's not about being trivial and frivolous, but ultimately about deepening our abandonment to God and his purposes for our wonderful world.

The material gathered here has grown out of many sources of playfulness in others. Primarily my family of children and grandchildren and their friends, but also from my work with those who are terminally ill, children with severe disability, those in prison, and people of other racial groupings. All these in many, many, situations of learning and training. Most of all, of course, it must have come from experiences of listening inside myself, and from my attempts to listen to God.

Please enjoy the book.

1

WHY NOW? WHY TODAY?

As a child, this is what I learnt by heart, in a very special sort of sing-song:

A wise man built his house upon a rock
and the rains came
and the floods came
and the winds *ble-e-e-e-e-e-e-e-e-e-ew . . .*
and *beat* upon that house –
AND IT FELL NOT, for it was founded on a rock.

A foolish man built his house upon the sand
and the rains came
and the floods came
and the winds *ble-e-e-e-e-e-e-e-e-e-ew . . .*
and beat upon that house –
and it *FELL . . .* (grand pause; and then triumphantly –)
and GREAT WAS THE FALL OF IT.

And this connected up with a well-loved story:

Once upon a time there were three little pigs.
The first little pig built a house with straw –
and the crafty old wolf, he huffed and he puffed
and he *ble-e-e-e-ew* the house down.
The second little pig built a house of wood –

and the crafty old wolf, he huffed and he puffed
and he *ble-e-e-e-ew* the house down.
The third little pig built a house of bricks –
and the crafty old wolf, he huffed and he puffed
and he *ble-e-e-e-ew*;
he huffed and he puffed and he *ble-e-e-e-ew*;
and he huffed and he puffed and he *ble-e-e-e-ew*;
AND THE HOUSE STOOD FIRM.

As we begin to explore the next millennium, we will want to make sure our house is built upon sound foundations. For most of us, our daily lives are so engrossing and it takes so much effort just to get through them, that looking at our foundations is a rare thing. It comes as a shock to find how shaky they have become. Some of those we tended to rely on during the last decades of the twentieth century are suspect. These are some of them:

- We developed a *Culture of Upness*.
  We had to be up-front and upwardly-mobile, keeping our end up to up-stage our competitors; we had to catch-up and mount-up and boot-up; to build-up and stay-up and show-up. What happened to stripping-down and centering-down and settling-down?
- We thought we suffered from *Time-Famine*.
  What happened to those lovely idling words like meandering, lingering, dawdling; the sort of low-intensity times of just being, and taking in? How often did we allow ourselves to enjoy a pootle day, or to luxuriate in simply lazing? Was it *really* necessary to be so urgently driven?
- We relied more and more on *Left-Brainitis*.
  Where did all those wonderful right-brain functions of dreaming and imagining, relaxing and just pondering go? Watching the

activities of Pooh and Piglet and Eeyore? Letting ourselves waft indecisively among the bluebells?

- Our priorities were to do with gaining *Control, and Certainty, and Comfort.*

  And so we expected our standard of living constantly to go on *up* – materially that is – and we lost sight of the things that grow between those who have less; of the freedom that can be part of risk; and of the creativity that emerges from conditions that are chaotic. We thought that places without comfort, which are beyond control, and hold no certainty, were no-go areas.

- Our leisure seemed to centre on *Rivalry, Violence, and Sex.*

  What happened to companionship, gentleness, courtship – those centuries-tried ways of behaving with courtesy, consideration, and good humour?

- Our culture was built on *Self-Responsibility, Accountability, Critical Analysis*; and its rewards were seen as *Status, Affluence, and High Consumption of Material Goods*.

  In themselves, all these are of course desirable. But on their own they are harsh, sharp, smart, and they veer towards being judgemental. Left alone they can bite and sting. And wherever people sense they are being judged they become defensive, and grow particularly crafty in throwing blame. Did you notice the pastime passion for planting Blame? Asking for 'heads to roll'? We commonly developed a nose for seeking out the weak spots of the other, to disclose and if possible amplify them. To make them public.

- Our taste in *humour was dire.*

  All those programmes about people falling over! And behaving badly; and pulling down reputations, and the lust for jibes and cynicism and obscenity. Most of it was at the cost of of someone else. Sometimes good humour disappeared altogether, and not just in the egotistical secular world. For some, the search after

> spirituality became intense. Gerard Hughes, the well-loved Jesuit guru, describes how as a young man 'there were times when I became spiritually over-heated, and could no longer laugh'.[1] A situation many could relate to.

If these are some of the foundations of the culture we built in the late twentieth century could we do differently now? We don't have to continue along the same lines, if we catch ourselves in time. What better chance to start changing our building styles than in a brand new millennium? We can learn from the past, but it doesn't have to hamper us as we step out today. We can plan for the future, but always in the knowledge that our plans may not work out as we imagine them. The only thing we really have to work with is the present moment. Our responses to *this* moment, *this* now, can be fresh and different because each new moment is unique, it has never happened in quite this way before. Hope and optimism depend on the reality of this truth – the present moment is always a new opportunity. The present is the last moment of my past and the first moment of my future: it's a pity to miss it.

WAYS AHEAD

Looking again at each of the tired attitudes listed above, there is one word that can revivify them all. It would loosen attitudes every time, add some elasticity, some fun. It would lessen the rigidity, the 'I'm always-right'-ness, the guardedness. The word would be – **playfulness**. It is a word wide open to new beginnings, because, according to a dictionary of word origins,[2] its genesis is obscure, and its ancestry is not fully accounted for, so it stands up in startling freshness. Playfulness is about story, laughter, song; fantasy, metaphor and surprise; it's about invention and dance and fluidity, and connects with words like tolerance and flexibility, acceptance and receptivity. These are all innate elements of playfulness, and they are all direct antidotes to the enveloping need for control, certainty and comfort. It's more about fun, than fret. It tries to turn *Being Driven* towards *Being Delighted*.

HOW CAN THIS RELATE TO PRAYER?

Whatever backdrop we have to our daily activity, it is bound to colour how we approach God. If we live in an atmosphere of busyness, seriousness, defendedness, self-consciousness, it is inevitable that it will affect the way we look at God. We can observe this in our public prayers: often they are peppered with demands – sometimes even feeling like commands – that we hand out to God. We don't notice any more how bossy we can get. We tell him (rather than suggest to him) to protect us; to send us peace; to make the other side see justice; to get things going our way. In so doing, we put all the responsibility on to God, and relieve ourselves of having to shoulder it, maybe because it is too heavy for us. At other times we find ourselves being craven: we wail 'we've failed again!' 'we're no good!' 'we're rotten through and through'. In a human parent–child relationship, this sort of language, persisted in, would prove to be disastrous. In human terms, it is well recognised that what really improves matters is when each person takes it on themselves to contribute something positive, reality-based, and lubricated with humour to a situation. Is that how we pray? Rejoicing at everyday events that show in God's love we can be hopeful, however preposterous things may seem? Do we affirm our belonging to the coming of the Kingdom of God?

There are some wonderful passages in the Old Testament describing God's desire for his people to celebrate the fact of belonging to him. Here is one of the less familiar stories:

> And Nehemiah and those that taught the people, said unto all the people, This day is holy unto the Lord your God; mourn not, nor weep . . . Go your way, eat the fat, drink the sweet, and send portions unto them for whom nothing is prepared: for this day is holy unto our Lord: neither be ye sorry; for the joy of the Lord is your strength.
>
> So the Levites stilled all the people, saying, Hold your peace, for the day is holy, neither be ye grieved.
>
> And all the people went their way to eat, to drink, and to send portions, and to make great mirth.
>
> And the leaders published and proclaimed in all their cities saying: Go forth unto the mount, and fetch olive branches and pine branches, and myrtle branches, and branches of thick trees, to make booths . . . So the people went forth, and brought them, and made themselves booths, every one upon the roof of his house, and in their courts, and in the courts of the house of God, and in the streets. And all the congregation made booths, and sat under the booths. And there was very great gladness.[3] (NJB 'there was very great merry-making.')

Imagine all the fun and good cheer and 'feel-good factor' that was generated by all that communal enjoyment. Many of the Judaic stories and prayers and songs that were inherited by Jesus bubble with joy and jokes and festive incongruities, and this earthy playfulness was carried through the early Christian Church. From the Middle Ages onward behaviour in Church grew increasingly solemn as our knowledge has become more serious and sophisticated. In our own century, the novelist/theologian/playwright Dorothy Sayers, commenting on the description in the Gospels of

Jesus being a 'wine-bibber and a glutton, a friend of publicans and sinners' says:

> For nineteen and a half centuries, the Christian Churches have laboured, not without success, to remove this unfortunate impression made by their Lord and Master. They have founded Total Abstinence Societies in the name of him who made the water wine, and added improvements such as bans and anathemas upon dancing and theatre-going. They have transferred the Sabbath from Saturday to Sunday, and, feeling the original commandment 'thou shalt not work' was rather half-hearted, have added to it a new commandment, 'thou shalt not play'. . . . The remarkable thing about it is its extreme unlikeness to the impression produced by Christ![4]

IN OUR OWN TIME

There is now a thriving movement to reintroduce play and humour into our Christian ministry. The organisations called 'Holy Fools' and 'Clowns for Christ' are becoming increasingly well known, working not only in chapels and churches and schools but hospitals and prisons. Much of this work has been spearheaded by Roly Bain, a priest who is also a highly regarded professional clown. In one of his books he writes:

> God has given us the possibility of dealing with our fallibility, not by feeling terribly guilty about it but by accepting it and laughing about it and transforming it. God's love is a liberating love with a redeeming smile. The love that is laughter is a gurgling, rumbling, irrepressible love that wells up from the

> very depths, is quite uncontrollable, irresistible, seems to split us in two. It leaves us changed and full of hope, having glimpsed something of another world, if not the eternal.[5]

FOLK PHILOSOPHY

Something else happened too. Since general standards of living started to improve in the 1970s, the folk philosophy of Doing the Best with What I've Got, has given way to What I Would Get if I Won the Lottery/Pools/Prize Draw/TV game. Doing the Best with What I've Got would often draw positively on inventiveness and imagination, humour and playfulness; and the feeling of beating the system at its own game piled on the self-esteem. Now, perhaps weekly, we put ourselves into the way of disappointment each time we lose what we've been hankering after, and this adds to the feeling of worthlessness and helplessness – or worse. There is no playfulness in being let down. But making the most of things as they are, instead of resenting them that they are not, can change things round.

There are new shoots sprouting.

In modern industry humour and playfulness are officially returning. They are being seen as management tools whereby the wellbeing of the workforce is increased, team cohesion is improved, and higher productivity levels are raised. *The Observer* headline 'Humour is the New Weapon in Business Wars'[6] is typical of a rash of articles appearing in the serious papers.

In health and healing today, it is recognised that laughter and play increase the efficiency of the immune system and speed up the healing process, both physically and psychologically. The first 'Laughter Clinic' in the National Health Service was set up by

Robert Holden[7] in the 1980s, and conferences and seminars have been set up by 'The Happiness Project' established at Oxford in the late 1990s. It presents the 'Happiness Principle' of 'Happychondria', and insists that everyone can be 'so Happy you almost feel guilty but not quite!'

In church culture a new mood is creeping into our poems and music and art. Stillness with God has expanded due to the practice encouraged by the Julian Meetings[8] and the Christian Meditation Centre.[9] Research has shown that those familiar with stillness laugh and play more than those to whom it is unfamiliar. Look at this poem: it's called 'Jeu d'Espirit'.

> Flame-dancing Spirit, come
> Sweep us off our feet, and
> Dance through our days.
> Surprise us with your rhythms.
> Dare us to try new steps, explore
> New patterns and new partnerships.
> Release us from old routines,
> To swing in abandoned joy and
> Fearful adventure.
> And in the intervals,
> Rest us,
> In your still centre.[10]

In many fields of human experience **playfulness** is seen as a direct antidote to the misguided emphases of so much of the late twentieth century. To rediscover this is the aim of the present book, chapter by chapter. It is not quite as simple as we might like it to be, and there is plenty of room for misunderstanding on the subject; but that is partly why it has become so neglected. The baseline of playfulness is trust and abandonment. It is about

mutual delight. As we go through the book there will be many aspects of play to look at. Getting to the bottom of what playfulness is suggests something that could be a profound recovery for the new millennium.

PERSONAL REFLECTION

We can end this chapter by playing on words (something which Jesus did to a surprising degree); this play isn't simply to be 'clever', but to bring out depths of meaning and interaction that wouldn't show up in any other way.

Dear God: in this very present moment, this here and now,
we present ourselves, just as we are,
to your presence; aware of
all the presents you long to lavish on us.
Be present to us. O Lord.

2

CHILDISHNESS AND CHILDLIKENESS

It's time to explore some of the words that will be used all through this book. In everyday speech, words like 'play' and 'playful' seem fairly interchangeable, but here they need to be unwrapped a bit. Similarly, in general conversation we are often unaware of any difference between 'childish' and 'childlike', yet for our present purpose it is important to understand their distinctiveness.

PLAY

This seems to be such an ordinary, simple, four-letter word. Perhaps it is significant – but it should be surprising – that there is no entry at all in *The Oxford Dictionary of the Christian Church* for 'play', 'playful', or 'playfulness'. The *Oxford English Dictionary*, however, has several quite separate interpretations. As we use it now, 'play' can refer to:

- a drama presented on a stage by people acting different parts;
- the act of making music on an instrument;
- the organised use of energy according to rules, as in hopscotch or football;
- something that is a diversion from work;
- being idle (!);

- anything coming from a middle Dutch word meaning 'dance, leap for joy, rejoice'.

PLAYING

When it comes to '**playing**', we are dealing with a surprisingly complicated notion. Playing can be carefree or regulated; affectionate or aggressive; solitary or competitive. It may be spontaneous or contrived; inviting or cruel; private or attention-seeking; sensitive or bullying. Then there is the term '**playing with**' and this is about manipulating something, whether it is words or objects or feelings; sometimes it can be according to rules but often it is not. These are complex ideas, but something strange happens when we look at '**playfulness**'.

PLAYFULNESS

Quite suddenly, without any warning, all these ideas change. There is little that is negative or complicated about being '*full*' of playfulness. It steps into another realm altogether. Playfulness is about letting down all the defences that are integral to play (just think of those rules and boundaries that are attached to any sport), and it moves straight into simplicity and trust and candour and acceptance. The *Dictionary of the Christian Church* does include the term 'plays', and its comment there is to do with 'passion'. True playfulness can only be built upon compassion.[1] Unkind play is indeed seen, for instance, in some playgrounds, but genuine playfulness can only thrive where the 'feeling-with' is mutual. Fear is absent. Playfulness doesn't detract from maturity or street-wisdom or intellect. A teacher who playfully joins in hopscotch with the

children doesn't lose their respect, and the professor being playful on the floor with the puppy is by no means seen as undignified. Playfulness adds to the richness of life, it doesn't discount anything. There is an important difference between activities that require some sort of intense self-consciousness, and *playfulness* which is free and unselfconscious. But it does mean letting go, temporarily, dropping off the skills and knowledge and sophistication that people usually take around with them. It's about being *totally welcoming and welcomed* – no holes barred.

Some of the traits of true playfulness are:

- being confident that it's okay to let go, and the other can too;
- being safe with the other; so safe that some of the certainties can float away, and it doesn't matter not-being-in-the-know just now;
- abandoning my own self-importance and marvelling with the one I'm playing with;
- catching an affront that has been thrown, but letting it slip off, without wasting energy on throwing it back;
- total absence of guile or malice; not even competitiveness gets in the way;
- going inside, and then giving the inside out; knowing I'm grubby and sometimes sore and often inadequate, but it doesn't matter because the one I'm playing with probably is too.

CHILDISHNESS AND CHILDLIKENESS

So what about the two words that are so alike – childish and childlike? Are there similar surprises to be found in them? Below is a table of words that attach themselves to either 'childish' or 'childlike'. What comes out of this comparison is illuminating.

Childishness	***Childlikeness***
immature	spontaneous, uncontrived
self-concerned, ego-centric	innocent – unselfconscious
attention-seeking	trusting
sulking	clear-minded, uncluttered
not getting what I want	receiving and giving delight
whining	
dissembling	open and filled with wonder
manipulative	unafraid of the intimacy of touch
scoring one against another	not concerned with 'winning'
taunting, teasing	enjoying mutual laughter
giggling	in the present moment
avoidance	safe
suppressed angst	relaxed, free of tension
insecure	gladness
bad at losing	
telling tales, spiteful	

A **childish** view of reality enables a person to deny what is obvious to others, while a **childlike** view of reality presupposes understanding. For instance:

> Jemima was very proud of the latest example of her jam-making skills. She hoped to introduce the new line – blackberry and rose petals – into her farm shop. Imagine her dismay when she discovered the jar half-empty and a sticky spoon left on the sideboard. She called her children, Jenny and Jane, from the garden. Jenny had traces of jam at the corners of her mouth and between her teeth. 'I didn't take any, I didn't, it was Jane,' she yelled, stamping her foot. Jane whispered, her finger in her

mouth, 'I just tasted it, Mum, so's I could tell you how yummy it is. Then I didn't tell you.' She wrapped herself around her mother's legs.

You only have to watch people playing in water – in a stream or at the seaside – to recognise the differences between childishness and childlikeness. Splashing others can be annoying or frightening, and it contrasts sharply with the shared squeals of spraying each other out of fun.

When it is applied to those who are no longer children, the word **childish** is almost always pejorative and somehow disapproving. It refers to behaviour that demands its own way without considering others, or behaviour that is blatantly approval-seeking. It is about being narked or miffed when I don't get want I want. Childishness often includes a form of self-delusion and a conviction that what is stated is true, whether it fits the facts or not. When the word **childlike** is applied to those who are no longer children, it may refer to an inappropriate innocence (which may be endearing) and naivety. More often it is about a characteristic of carefree trust and engaging spontaneity, one that is not threatened by change, a freedom from conventional constraints, unphased by appearing to be made a fool of, uncompetitive, disconnected from any concern with judgement.[2]

MEETING OTHERS

When I meet something or someone I love, or that I want to love me, my immediate concern is to try to get into play.

A tickle behind the dog's ears
Or under the cat's chin
A finger caress that produces a smile or a giggle from the baby
A gesture that says 'I'm safe, you're safe, let's delight each other'
The spark that jumps between two people at a party

But when I meet up with *God* – my head goes down, my eyes dutifully close, I remember my sins, and I take on a reverential, deferential, grave and staid attitude. *What would you have to say about it if your child did that to you?*

I can also be playful on my own. A letter came from a friend which described her depression bordering on despair. Then, she writes, 'I took a bath, and lying back, I created shapes in the bubbles. Finding a very lifelike squirrel looking cheekily at me out of the froth was a great surprise. "You didn't expect me to be here, did you?" it said, and scampered off. It was about that uninhibited joy in discovery and meeting that all young children – and of course animals – have, but from which we adults have become immunised.' The letter continues, 'Phew! I feel a whole heap better now.'

Maybe it's something to do with what Hildegard of Bingen[3] calls 'accepting the abundance of spiritual gladness'.

FROM THE GOSPELS

Some of these observations may help to make Jesus' claims that we all, young, middle-aged and elderly, have to 'be as little children', a little clearer. The following are two contrasting versions of Luke 9:46–8.[4] First, as it is translated in the New Revised Standard Version:

> An argument arose among them as to which one of them was the greatest. But Jesus, aware of their inner thoughts, took a little child and put it by his side, and said to them, 'Whoever welcomes this child in my name welcomes me, and whoever welcomes me welcomes the one who sent me: for the least among all of you is the greatest.'

And the recent American paraphrase of the Bible by Eugene Peterson, called *The Message*, puts it like this:

> They started arguing over which of them would be most famous. When Jesus realized how much this mattered to them, he brought a child to his side. 'Whoever accepts this child as if the child were me, accepts me,' he said. 'And whoever accepts me accepts the One who sent me. You become great by accepting, not asserting. Your spirit, not your size, makes the difference.'

It can be even more revealing to look at how Jesus behaved towards adults who were acting in child-mode. Several incidents in the Gospels, where one might expect a grown-up adult to be rebuffed by the adult Jesus, are written with illuminating responses.

(a) When James and John come to Jesus asking him if they can 'sit on his right hand for ever' it would seem to us to be positively childish behaviour with its mixture of naivety, self-disclosure, self-concern. It would seem to call for a stern put-down in a distinctly parental voice, but Jesus meets it with great gentleness and tact, using images of baptism. He discerns, and refers to, the deeply insecure childlike place from which the request came. [Matthew 20:23; Mark 10:35–40; Luke 9:46–7]

(b) The story of Thomas which concerns the physical wounds of Jesus shows a stubbornness linked with curiosity that is childlike. The doubt and lack of trust that he showed could have brought out a very strict rebuff from Jesus, but once again it is met with a sure acceptance of the child in Thomas, and an invitation whose welcome has reverberated across the centuries. The child's need for reassurance and touch was drawn upon by Jesus as a way of re-establishing their relationship of love. [John 20:24–8]

(c) Then there is the extraordinary incident where the exhausted disciples, having wrestled all night with their fishing nets and used all their local knowledge, tried yet again at the request of 'a stranger'. Were they being mild, or sullen and resentful? Or were they tied into a basic childish/childlike obedience? However they were feeling, it was rewarded by a prepared breakfast beach barbecue, and an over-abundance of fish. Surely a source of great laughing! [John 21:3–13]

(d) Perhaps there was one occasion where child-mode spontaneity was repelled by Jesus. Following straight on the euphoria of the Transfiguration, Peter blurted out his need to capture this

> supreme event. He was off his guard, unperceptive, and immediate to his own feelings as a child wanting to cling on and not go forward. Jesus' response was sharp and imperative – he saw the wiles of the devil contaminating the scene and felt the power of his own past temptations in the desert. 'Get thee behind me, Satan,' he demanded. [Matthew 16:23; Mark 8:33; Luke 11:18]

The issue that shines through all these examples is Jesus' receptivity to the child that is in each of us. Educated and sophisticated as we feel we are these days, when another grown-up displays their childishness the impulse of adults is to 'put them down' or 'show them up'. We feel we have a duty to reveal their un-adultness, we want to snuff the child out of them. We have to prove how superior we are to childlikeness, something we have 'put behind' us. Is that *really* a welcoming, healing, appropriate, necessary response?

PERSONAL REFLECTION

Does my own inner child become neglected, put down, smothered, ignored, unloved when I get 'grown up'? Could it be that in this way I sell myself short? Look at it like this poet:

The Prayer of the Goat[5]

Lord!
I need a little wild freedom,
a little giddiness of heart,
the strange taste of the unknown flowers.
For whom else are Your mountains?
Your snow wind? These springs?

The sheep do not understand.
They graze and graze,
all of them,
and always in the same direction,
and then eternally chew the cud.
But I – I love to bound to the heart of all
Your marvels,
leap Your chasms,
and, my mouth stuffed with intoxicating grasses,
quiver with an adventurer's delight
on the summit of the world!

Carmen Bernos de Gasztold

3

JESUS AND THE CHILDREN

The subject of Jesus and the children is absorbing. He had such a strong affinity with them. To understand something of how this grew let's stretch our imaginations a little and look at the sort of experience he himself had as a child. We have very little in the way of factual records to go on, but if we bring to them our own experience of what it is like to be a child, that limited record might light up for us.

JESUS AS A CHILD HIMSELF

To start with the obvious: Joseph was a mature master craftsman, with a practice on one of the main trading routes through Palestine. There would have been plenty of calls for him to repair carts, axles, and carriage wheels. Luggage boxes and shepherds' crooks would have been popular items for him to sell, and local people must have appreciated his house furniture. So by contemporary standards the family was reasonably well provided for and held in respect by the neighbourhood. Customers, both new and known, would have dropped in for a chat, and in all likelihood Joseph joked and laughed with them in the way that confident craftsmen do all over the world. Jesus would watch, listen and help wherever possible.

The only Gospel reference we have of Jesus between the ages of two and twelve is this:

> When they had done everything the law of the Lord required, they went back to Galilee, to their own town of Nazareth. And as the child grew to maturity, he was filled with wisdom; and God's favour was with him. (Luke 2:39–40 NJB)[1]

We don't know if Jesus grew up with brothers, and maybe sisters, or whether his 'brethren' James and John were cousins, but it is clear that he lived in a circle of other children. Jesus was a *real* child of grazed knees, tears, varying moods, and laughter. In spite of the well-loved pictures we have inherited, it is improbable that he was the child of golden curls and white nightgowns that so many hold in their imaginations. It is a very useful exercise to sit back and prise open some of the stereotyping that is common among us: Jesus must have had, to say the least, a pretty unusual childhood, and maybe we should be prepared for some surprises.

- What was Jesus' personal experience of childhood in Nazareth really like? Was he the brunt of village gossip? The unusual facts about the engagement of Mary and Joseph, and that he hadn't 'put her away' in accordance with local custom, would be food for gossip for generations in a society without newspapers or television or cinema. And all the stories about dreams and visions, armies of angels in the sky, visits from foreign moguls, infant massacres and midnight escapes would have been marvellous sources for story-telling around the evening fires. What sort of 'playfulness' fitted this?
- Jesus must have been an extraordinarily aware and sensitive child, highly observant of all the activity about him, both in the natural world and in human behaviour. Such a child would attract attention from other parents, who would compare his development with that of their own, less gifted, children. How did the parents of the rest of his group advise their sons to treat him? Was he held up as an example, or were his peers

encouraged to 'pull him down a peg'? 'Good' children are not necessarily always liked. Jesus as a boy may have been mischievous, but never deliberately hurtful. For instance, did he ever fight back, when other boys accosted him? How did he respond when he was 'dared' to steal, or begged to lie to protect his fellows? Maybe he would have been excluded from 'the gang', even bullied and ostracised for being extra caring. As children will be children, Jesus would know what it is like to be snubbed, to be put down; and perhaps he would discover how much you can learn about yourself as you lick your wounds. It may have been incidents like this that enabled him to grow in resilience and independence in thought.

- How did he cope with the usual temptations of all children to test boundaries of 'good' behaviour? At some time in their development, most young boys are goaded by their peers to flaunt the values of adults, to test them out for themselves. What did Jesus do in such a situation? In his adult life Jesus was continually pushing out the boundaries of conventional accepted law-abiding behaviour. Where did that confident ability start?
- Most probably he knew all about teasing and being teased. Did he learn about the uses of 'teasing' humour from his childhood? In adulthood his ability to play with words, to banter using one position and then another, was used to great effect. The witticisms he threw out to attract the attention of the crowds, the quick responses he used to parry the rapier thrusts of intellectuals who were out to trap him, the playful to-and-froing of verbal teasing with which he engaged the Samaritan woman at the well and also the distracted Syro-Phoenician mother, are all examples of a skill he must have begun to learn in childhood.[2] He did not get it from books or the theatre or university.
- Just as Jesus spent time in the countryside, learning about the

ways of shepherds and sowers, hens and larks and sparrows, lilies and corn, he also spent time watching the children playing in the market-place. The unco-operative behaviour of children who refused to join in with the games, whether these were sad or happy, was an unsatisfactory experience for him. Was he 'watching' from the edges of the play from his own choice? Or was he excluded? Or was it simply that he preferred to be on his own?

✤ Wherever it came from, whether it was from some particular incident he experienced himself or from watching others, Jesus developed a deep horror towards those who wished harm to children.[3] The strong and personal dismay he expressed in adulthood at those who put obstacles in the way of a child, particularly 'one who believes', may reflect something he met in his own personal experience in childhood. Maybe he had a special access to their fragility due to attitudes he had had to deal with himself.

JESUS AS A TEENAGER

✤ When the twelve-year-old boy Jesus visited the golden temple in Jerusalem it was an event of enormous significance. Firstly, it was his initiation into adulthood; it was the growing boy's first taste of large crowds, wide culture, deep learning, and it whet his appetite for all three. Secondly, it portrays his absorption in religious experience and understanding. Thirdly, it is a story about the extended community and how Mary and Joseph could be unconcerned even though their son wasn't physically in their sight – he would probably be involved with others in the group as it travelled. As important as any of these things, the story tells us about the relationship that Jesus thought he had with his parents, but which they didn't recognise. As the young Jesus sat for three days with the elders of the temple, listening and learning and voicing his own ideas to them, there must have come a time when they wondered who was going to feed him, and where he was going to sleep. Something about Jesus' confidence that his parents *knew where he would be*, that he assumed they *would understand he had to be about his Father's business*, and would naturally know where to find him, must have been strong enough to convince them they needn't have any anxiety on this account. Jesus obviously took for granted that his parents would understand, and this assumption was built upon his experience of living with them until that time. And yet Mary and Joseph themselves were fraught with anxiety when they realised he wasn't with their friends. They went from place to place, house to house, until eventually after three days they thought of looking for him in the temple. What did this lack of comprehension do to a loving son? More than anything, perhaps this was the beginning of his separated adulthood.

In spite of this, Jack Dominian[4] traces the security and maturity of Jesus' relationship with his mother and father all through his development. Without a firm foundation of love and laughter, Jesus would have been unable as an adult to be

- as strong as he was, while accepting the weakness of others, as he did;
- as courageous as he was, while able to display the full effects of grief and dismay and anger and longing, as he did;
- as radical as he was, while understanding the need of others to rely on structures, as he did;
- and Jesus must have learnt trust and abandonment and playfulness with his family, or his future relationship with children, and

hosts, and marginalised people could never have been as rich as it was.

THE ADULT JESUS WITH THE CHILDREN

The references to Jesus' relationship with children run right through the Gospels like an undercurrent, always there but peaking at certain specific points. He felt not only affection for children (he put his arms around them[5]), but pity ('Daughters of Jerusalem . . . weep rather for yourselves and your children'[6]) and respect ('wisdom has been proved right by all her children'[7]).

> People brought babies for him to touch, and when the disciples saw them they rebuked them. But Jesus called for the children and said, 'Let the children come to me; do not try to stop them; for the kingdom of God belongs to such as these. Truly I tell you: whoever does not accept ["welcome in" NJB] the kingdom of God like a child will never enter it.' (AV)[8]

✤ At other times Jesus' great tenderness is translated into the phrase 'these little ones'. When he expresses the full vent of his feelings against those who 'despise', 'offend', 'harm', 'allow to perish', 'place a stumbling block in the way of . . .'[9] children, he uses this peculiarly empathetic phrase. Perhaps it tells us most about Jesus' concern for children when he teaches his disciples that 'in heaven, their angels do always behold the face of my Father which is in heaven'; and 'it is not the will of your Father . . . that one of these little ones should perish' (AV).[10] These words reveal the closeness Jesus kept with children even when his ministry was chiefly about interrelating with adults.

- Other observations by Jesus of the children around him are recorded as times of joy when they shouted 'Hosanna',[11] of discord when they rebelled from their parents,[12] of play in the market-place,[13] and of their presence at the huge meetings where several thousand were fed – indeed these feedings were only made possible by the provisions simplistically offered by a small boy.[14] And then, of course, there were the healings. The daughter of the Canaanite woman who, in spite of her grief, used her wits to engage Jesus in word-play;[15] the son of the man who took him to the powerless disciples, but from whom Jesus dispelled the wild spirit and then 'put him on his own two feet';[16] the daughter of Jairus, a leader from the synagogue, whom the neighbours thought dead but when Jesus held her hand he lifted her up asking for food to be brought to her;[17] and the royal official from Capernaum, whose son Jesus healed from a distance.[18] Jesus' experience with children as an adult was varied and comprehensive; it is interesting that his *play* with them is not seen as necessary to record.

JESUS' LOVE OF CHILDREN APPLIED TO ADULTS

The phrase 'the children of God' to describe those who are seeking the will of their Creator is not familiar in the Old Testament, but Jesus makes use of it constantly.[19] It is an important image to him, and one that is taken up by his closest biographer, John. On several occasions he calls his disciples his 'children'.[20] This longing love of Jesus to enfold and nurture all those he cares for is expressed even as he approaches his passion. Looking down on the city of Jerusalem spread out below him, it's almost as if he catches his breath in the cry 'O Jerusalem, Jerusalem, city that murders the prophets and stones the messengers sent to her! How often have I longed to gather your children, as a hen gathers her brood under her wings; but you would not let me.'(REB)[21]

THE WHOLE EFFECT

As far as we know, as an adult Jesus was without a close family of his own. Yet he valued highly his ability to share with children their experience of pain, grief, joy and play. This must have come from a strong desire to stay connected to what it is like to be a child, and never to throw out the child within. The variety of the times he was with children *where they were* instead of where the adults thought they ought to be, speak of a direct empathy between their child's experience and his own. The very fact that he was able to be with them in their confusion and sickness and fragility, enabled them to respond by being open to him in exuberance and trust and playfulness.

The children came to him, and he put his arms around them, because they knew he understood.

> He folded and blessed them and gave each one their say
> And we saw Christ's laughing face all that day.
> Blessed were the children who answered his call.
> And blessed is the child's heart alive in us all.[22]

PERSONAL REFLECTION

Do I struggle to 'snuff out' the child in me? Even worse, do I do my best to snub the child in others?

By denying the feelings of the child within me, am I truncating or even obliterating something that can free me up to play? Have I forgotten to value playfulness in my everyday living, or in others, or worse still in my approach to God my Father? What is it about simplicity, trust, and inexperience that makes me feel shamed? Can I learn to love the child in me a bit more, play with the child more, welcome that child more?

4

PLAY, LAUGHTER, AND WONDER: SOME OF THE FACTS

There are stories of the prophet David, as he exulted in the goodness of God, dancing and playing before the ark of the Lord having uncovered all his defences and stripped himself of his clothing.[1] What a metaphor! Playfulness, laughter and wonder all spring out of the desire to *let go*: to strip off my precious self-image, let down the barriers, and drop the defendedness which so often gets in the way of relating freely. Until I'm brave enough to let go, the way I relate to anything will be tight and tied up; and this will be so whether it is about relating to my real self, or to others, or to God.

If only we would believe in our own beliefs; if only we spent time looking at the *grounds* for our own playfulness. The Bible holds a great many warnings, but far above these is the constant recurring theme of 'do not fear', and 'be of good cheer'. This glad reassurance occurs more, in both Old and New Testaments, than any reference to anxiety or guilt. Running through the whole is a continuous stream of praise and joyfulness and a throwing away of self-engrossed protectiveness. For instance, look at some of the expressions of well-grounded gladness we have been given in Isaiah:

Sing, barren woman who never bore a child; break into a shout

> of joy, you that have never been in labour; for the deserted wife will have more children than she who lives with her husband, says the Lord. Though the mountains may move and the hills shake, my love will be immovable and never fail. (54:1, 10 REB)

> Rejoice with Jerusalem and exult in her, share her joy with all your heart. Her babes will be carried in her arms and dandled on her knees; as a mother comforts her son so shall I myself comfort you. At the sight your heart will be glad, you will flourish like grass in spring. (66:10–13 REB)

In good times and distressing times, God's love and companionship never falters. Our own experience of dismay is eased if, just sometimes, we can let in this exultation.

PHYSIOLOGY

It is built into the blueprint of our creation that we have a two-fold nervous system. One system enables us to respond to challenge, alarm, or stimulation; it gets us going and enables us to achieve and top up our goals, doing things as fast and as well and impressively as we can. It is competitive and exciting (while we feel we can keep up) and most of our living today is based on this activity. It is known as the sympathetic nervous system, and is laid out like a telephone network all over our bodies and brains. The basic communication is made by means of a constellation of enzymes based on adrenaline.

What is less well known is that we are also equipped with an alternative network, using a counter group of enzymes, which is called the parasympathetic nervous system. In contrast to the striving nature of the sympathetic system, behaviour in the parasympathetic mode is relaxed, playful, healing, meditative. It is by contacting this system – sometimes quite deliberately – that my body relaxes, heals quicker, builds up its immunity to disease, breathes less anxiously, laughs more easily, and takes on playfulness. And putting myself in the way of this wonderful state is something I can *choose*.

PHILOSOPHY

In her persuasive book Rebecca Abrams tells us that God is, above all, 'a playful God, reminding us that play is at the heart of creation and re-creation, both divine and human.'[2] She goes so far as to say that what makes some kinds of behaviour highly rewarding, and others profoundly tedious, is the degree of play in them. An American psychologist Aric Sigman has written that 'Humans are born into bodies that are designed to feel good as a primary mode of being . . . to experience the tingling pulse of embodied spirit that should come so easily to humans'.[3] When we think of the appalling pictures on our screens of the play-deprived orphans in Romania we come to realise that play is something of great profundity. And yet for centuries we have been led to believe that play is something to be left behind as early as possible, and that any self-respecting adult should put it very low on their agenda. Almost without being aware of it, we have allowed playfulness to seem childish, lazy, irresponsible and immoral. Instead we have taken on a philosophy of continuously trying harder. Self-improvement has become our chief driver. 'Improvement' has inflated itself to such a degree it is now a social bugbear.[4]

Playfulness is about *not trying*; it is about being whoever we are *now*, and celebrating just that for the moment. Letting ourselves off the hook just for a few seconds. Getting away from all that intense seriousness. It makes it possible to recoup some energy for the next stint.

We have forgotten that we actually suffer when we cannot or do not play. Our modern culture at work is one of instability, uncertainty and anxiety. Add to that those who care for others and put themselves last, and the way they feel they have to wage war with the urge to play. An emphasis on self-improvement and self-consciousness now seems a mirror we carry around inside us, continually reflecting back every thought and decision. It tries to make unselfconscious playfulness virtually impossible.

To take it even further, recent studies have shown that adults whose behaviour is anti-social or even criminal are the very ones who have been seriously deprived of play as children. Fortunately, this negation of the value of play is at last beginning to change.

LAUGHTER

We have already taken a brief look at how fun and laughter are being reintroduced into industry and health, church and academia.[5] We are being told increasingly that laughter is good for us.

- Smiling and laughing use fewer muscles than frowning and rowing
- Smiling and laughing activate the parasympathetic nervous system, and all its accompanying benefits
- Smiling and laughing increase the production of pain-relieving hormones; they add to the feel-good factor in a way that is contagious

- We can all do it: like running, it comes naturally, without even trying, but we can forget how to do it through neglect
- Babies who are born deaf and dumb chuckle and laugh: even they, on their own, with no external stimulation, can be happily merry
- When I am laughing, I am practising internal aerobics
- When I am laughing, I am not fighting

But it does very much depend on what sort of laughter it is we are enjoying.[6]

Here is a small story:

> It was at a laughter workshop being run for a community of nuns. Among those attending, there was a Sister who had been professed all her life, and she was ninety-six. For seventy-eight years she had been clothed in black from the top of her head to the soles of her feet. Now, the well-loved guru of her community, her body was wizened, and she sat all that day in the corner, bowed and silent. The leader of the workshop talked about the differences between head laughter, heart laughter, and laughter which wells up from the centre, the belly. The figure in the corner leapt up: 'Ah!' she said. 'Belly laughter! Belly laughter is *good*'!

Laughter based on the intellect, on something contained in my knowledge and coming from the head, can be witty and ironic, cynical and sarcastic, clever and superior, or snide and mocking. It is not necessarily 'good'.

Laughter based on the emotions, on something coming from the heart, can be affectionate and warm, or anxious, cruel, scorning and even stigmatising. It is not necessarily 'good'.

But laughter that wells up from the belly is wholesome, contagious, inclusive, welcoming. It is not *at* anything or anybody, but *with* them, alongside them. It is wholly 'good'. As we shall see later, it can indeed be holy. It is said of a Buddhist monastery that the monks, having meditated silently for an hour daily, come out into the courtyard with gales of laughter. When Jesus saw the eminent personage Zacchaeus perched up in the tree, what sort of laughter would have exploded from him? Would it have been at or with him? Would it have been a companioning, disarming, uniting sort of laughter?

WONDER

This is a word full of amazement, full of things beyond my understanding, of an astounded letting-go of all that is known. A word seldom heard today except as a mild query – 'I wonder . . .' – its power and glory has been degraded, down-sized, the dumbing effect of true wonder laid aside. It seems as though the more we think we know and the more we think we are in control the less we feel the need to wonder. But increasingly the leading physicists are saying there is more out there than even they can conceive of, and many of our concepts of being in control are turning into fantasy. Letting-go and playfulness are essential ingredients of wonder.

> Here the sun stands, and knows not East or West;
> Here no tide runs.
> We have come, last and best, from the wide zone
> Through dizzying circles hurled
> To that still centre, where the spinning world
> Rests on its axis.
>
> Dorothy L. Sayers

Allied to wonder is story-telling. Sometimes things that cannot be

expressed in prosaic terms can be held together in a story, or understood through allegory. There is a vigorous new interest in story-telling today that is reintroducing us to wonder.

PRAYER

Prayer can be about letting go and letting in playfulness and laughter and wonder and story-telling. It has been described by Henri Nouwen like this:

> Prayer is the bridge between my unconscious and conscious life. Prayer connects my mind with my heart, my will with my passions, my brain with my belly. Prayer is the way to let the Spirit of God penetrate all the corners of my being. Prayer is the divine instrument of my wholeness, unity, and . . . a presence deeper and wider than my senses can contain.[7]

Tom Wright adds:

> It is not a matter of a Christian grabbing a whim that comes into mind, sending up a casual prayer, and having it granted. When Jesus talks about 'in my name', he means 'in my character' . . . He wants us to do and be all that we are intended to do and be. The only way we will accomplish that is through constant prayer. We must pray for the work of God in us and through us, pray for the glory of God to be seen in us and through us, pray for the love of God to shine in us and through us.[8]

PERSONAL REFLECTION

Prayer is not primarily about telling God what he should do about the world – he already has his plans and purpose in mind; nor even about reminding him of what I am feeling now – he has a good idea of that too. When I pray I am choosing to align myself totally with him and his will and desire and longings for this his beautiful but wayward world. Unlike the children in the market-place, what he is pleased with I would be pleased about too; what he weeps over I would weep over too. Most of all I would marvel that he has wanted me to be at one with him: astonishment upon wonder upon marvel . . .

Perhaps all these aspects are summed up in a prayer of Charles de Foucauld:

> Father, I abandon myself into Your hands,
> Do with me whatever You will.
> Whatever You may do, I thank You.
> I am ready for all, I accept all.
> Let only Your will be done in me,
> and in all Your creatures.
>
> Into Your hands I commend my spirit.
> I offer it to You with all the love that is in my heart.
> For I love You, Lord, and so want to give You myself,
> to surrender myself into Your hands,
> without reserve and with boundless confidence,
> for You are my Father.
>
> Amen.

5

WHY SHOULD ADULTS *WANT* TO PLAY?

God is at home, it is we who have gone for a walk.

Meister Eckhart

And to where, in our adult sophistication, did we walk off?

In the process of growing up, of becoming adult, things may happen unawares.

Firstly, we may find we do quite well for ourselves, and a form of stable self-expectation or complacency sets in. Things are okay as they are, and we don't really want to put energy into thinking how they could be different.

Alternatively, whether we do well or do badly, we arrive at a place where we are holding down suppressed anger that things aren't better than they are. Anger is essentially the emotion that turns up when I don't see things going my way. It can revamp itself as anxiety or blame; most of us carry with us a degree of worry or of allocating fault that we don't want to see. Blame is inefficient, it is often unreal, and it usually aggravates the fight. Anxiety and blame both distance me from playfulness. That distance, which is similar to the distance between childlikeness and adulthood, gets filled up with differing priorities.

As we establish ourselves as adults, we dress ourselves up in status and possessions; we disguise ourselves behind coping styles; we scaffold ourselves by our achievements and reputation.

It is hardly surprising that we don't really want to let go of it all. We don't want to be stripped of what we think we are, back to who we really are. When we feel over-pressed, with too much to do, too many demands to be met, altogether too heavily laden, we want to get out, but not to change.

Often we will try to meet an excess of burden by an excess of something that we imagine will bring release. Sometimes it takes the form of fierce competition in sport; or it may be in the form of raised levels of noise; or of excess in drugs, drink, or sex. In overdoing it at one end of the scale we persuade ourselves to overdo it at the other.

Barry Wimbolt[1] points up 'the lies we tell ourselves just to get through the day, arguing my own justifications of myself, filtering the things I want myself to know, kidding myself to such an extent I don't even recognise I'm doing it'. So we become conditioned to unawareness and denial, and as unaware adults we lack the very feelings, perceptions and acumen we need to understand the depth and enormity of our dilemma.[2] We go to courses and workshops to talk about how to deal with others – but talk less about how we deal with what's inside ourselves. What is happening?

There was a remarkable woman who worked between World War I and II at writing, painting and thinking. She was a distinguished psychoanalyst named Marion Milner. In her late twenties she decided to give up depending on other people's approval, to get below the noisy clamouring of her will and the social norms expected of her, and to make contact with her own deepest needs. She noted, 'I want a chance to play; to do things I choose just for the joy of doing, for no purpose of achievement.' She realised the more she crammed her life with activity and experience, the more frustrated she felt. And the less she *strove* after happiness and contentment, the more she seemed to find. She began to let go, noting again, 'Why had no one told me that the function of the will might be to stand back, to wait, to stop pushing?' When she did let go, she found the simplest tasks were meaningful, and the hardest, simple. Boring chores became fluid and satisfying when she stopped her brain from interfering and allowed her arm to do them. It was the same when she played ping-pong; having been brought up to believe that to try was the only way of overcoming difficulty, she would concentrate, frowning with the effort, and she then found that this only stiffened her body. When she experimented instead with relaxing, her arm seemed to know what to do by itself.[3]

Of course we need to hold on to our maturity: that programme of knowledge, experience and skills that we have taken so much trouble to acquire. But there are times when both we, and others, can get out of the nightmare of having to stay perpetually in control, and ditch the need to interfere, and to help, and to correct.[4] We can let ourselves put it all on one side just for a while and once again meet the God who is at home, and to recover the gaiety and mirth, delight and playfulness he offers us.

HOW?

Now, just stop and think: *What do you most enjoy doing with a child who is special to you?* As parent, aunt, uncle, friend, what have been the greatest moments you spent together? Having meals? Parties? Teaching them something new? Going to church? Praying with them? Or *playing*? This is a very strange, and funny, thing: have you noticed that the difference between playing and praying is a matter of whether the second stroke 'l' stands up straight or bends over? This apparently trivial fact can trigger an important metaphor. When I prepare to pray to God, do I tend to lower my head and bend over, hiding my face and modestly disguising how

Pray

and

Play

I really feel? If this position is one that helps me to focus and concentrate, then that is all to the good. But if it is habitual and unthinking it can do insidious damage. Jesus himself probably prayed standing upright, like his fellow Jews at prayer, full face to God, but for many it is a real difficulty to be who they really are as they approach God. Someone said recently, 'When you stopped telling me what to do, it brought me into reality.' God loves us at each moment for the person we actually are, not for what we might eventually – after a great deal of struggle – become. The theologian David Pailin has put it like this:

> The freedom of theistic faith does not require people to pretend to be other than they are. The quiet person is under no obligation to try to be a jolly member of the fellowship; the questioning person does not have to feel guilty about doubting; the humorist does not have to act in a staid manner; the

emotional person does not have to try to adopt a stiff upper lip – nor the reserved person to let his or her feelings show.[5]

Standing upright in front of a mirror, and praying out loud some of the playful psalms (for instance those quoted in this book), perhaps even with appropriate body gestures, can bring us in touch with the grace of playing before God. Soon it may become unselfconscious.

We are told that the twelfth-century saint Mechtilde of Magdeburg wrote: *'I, God, am your playmate! I will lead the child in you in wonderful ways for I have chosen you.'*[6]

GOD WANTS ME AS HIS PLAYMATE!

At a series of workshops with this title, participants were asked to write down the characteristics they most valued in their childhood playmate. The following terms are what they came up with:

having fun together
sharing secrets
imaginative make-believe games
exploring with me
laughing together
always available
happy nature
right for me
longed to be together
exclusiveness
someone always there

companionship
excitement to be around
loved their company
being silent together
dressing-up, preparing for the adult world
seeking each other out
knowing when I was unhappy
doorways were opened into the security and stability of other families

never knowing what would happen next
enjoying the same things
comfortable and comforting
liked to be on my side
accepting me whatever
risked defying authority with me!
didn't have to try too hard
just sparked me off
just being together, not doing very much

How do these characters reflect my own relationship with God?

You may like to pause at this point to take a few minutes to look carefully at the words above, discovering where they match up with your own experience with the God who made you.

THE CHILD-OF-GOD ADULT

There are people – there have been two or three in my life – who stand out like beacons in the dark. People whose first mark is one of gentleness, who know so deeply that they are loved that they can totally dispose of impressing others. Their conviction of being loved is so secure that they have nothing to prove, and they throw self-importance to the winds. Laughter and playfulness, wonder and prayer are as real in them as blood and bone. Words like simplicity and humility come to mind, but these are over-worked in the spiritual vocabulary, maybe gladness and non-possessiveness are nearer. Acutely conscious of the tragedies of the world, they don't seem to be pulled down by them. Hope is so real, that somehow their deep human empathy for suffering doesn't burden them. St Francis of Assisi is perhaps the best-known icon of this blend of pain-knowing carried with light. It is something that doesn't even try to make an impact. It is caught, not taught. Talking to such rare people, you feel it is a spring morning and the buds are bursting, the birds are in full throttle, and the fox-cubs are bouncing. It is a Jesus quality. When you have met it you never forget it.[7]

This form of playfulness is not about excess, it is not related to overdoing it. It is not about extrovert excitement. Its wellsprings are set deeply in stillness, the place at the centre of all things where I know I am accepted, forgiven, loved, just as I am. That God-given assuredness that all shall be well, and all shall be well, and all manner of things shall be well however grubby, or scarred, or inept I happen to be.

THEORETICAL BACKGROUND

Psychological studies have been made comparing the effects of three separate degrees of high points in life. Three technical terms have been identified:

(i) **peak experience**, which includes ecstasy;

(ii) **peak performance**, which includes that level of our functioning which exceeds our typical behaviour; and

(iii) **flow**, an experience found in play and enjoyment, and one that is intrinsically rewarding because it 'flows' primarily for itself, with no conscious outcome. Flow stands outside boredom, anxiety and guilt. It doesn't necessarily entail intensity of feelings or superior performance. Flow is fun; it is interactive and involves fusion with another and thus a loss of self-consciousness. It is often the means of renewing those people and activities that have tended to become apathetic or alienated.[8] Enthusiasm, which could be sacred or festive as is appropriate, and even feelings of exaltation are followed by easy laughter and relaxation.

IN RELATIONSHIPS

This concept of **flow** has an added dimension. In our close relationships, and especially in our intimate relationships, there are times when the attitude of one or another becomes critical, exacting, legalistic. We are all imperfect, and none of us can stand up to this sort of scrutiny, although we may frequently indulge ourselves in applying it to others. Sotile has a wonderful alternative picture of getting on with each other. He suggests 'the meandering that is often necessary to keep up comfortable connections with those closest to you' because this enables us to 'tolerate the differences that there are between people'.[9] For example, we can learn to savour in an unhasty and unflurried way books, and gardens, and relationships. Letting them flow. And when things get really bad it can help to play a game called 'In It Together'. It doesn't really matter who is 'right'. It loses all importance once it's possible to say – with Anthony de Mello – 'I'm an ass, and you're an ass. We'll go along as asses together.'[10] Or as someone said to me recently, 'If there's a row, we just agree that he's an old goose and I'm an old goat so who is top doesn't matter a scrap, it doesn't come into it, it's irrelevant.' And the flow can get on with flowing. It can be a remarkably effective way of closing an argument or even a row, and restarting the flow.

> There were two teams rowing in a race. Team A were working hard as individuals, each member of the crew putting their all into the effort and tension of doing their best. Each wanted to win, to be top, to be first. The intensity was colossal. The enormous strain on each was evident in their faces, their shoulders, their bodies. They lost the race.
>
> Team B wanted to win too, but they flowed together as a

team. The entire crew melded into the common effort, swinging together in action. The movement was relaxed and purposeful and strong, their muscles rippling in unison. Each face watched the others, expressions flowing towards a common goal. They won the race.

The diagram on p. 48 can be useful in helping each one of us discover which bits of our lives include flow, and how perhaps we could let loose more of it. We *can* do it: I can do it and you can do it, if only we want to.

PERSONAL REFLECTION

Genuine playfulness grows out from a centre of stillness. As one participant remarked having shared in a playfulness meditation: '*Problems cease to have such a hold on you because you begin to share – to glimpse – God's perspective; and he's there with you to deal with it.*'

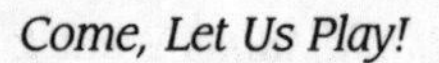

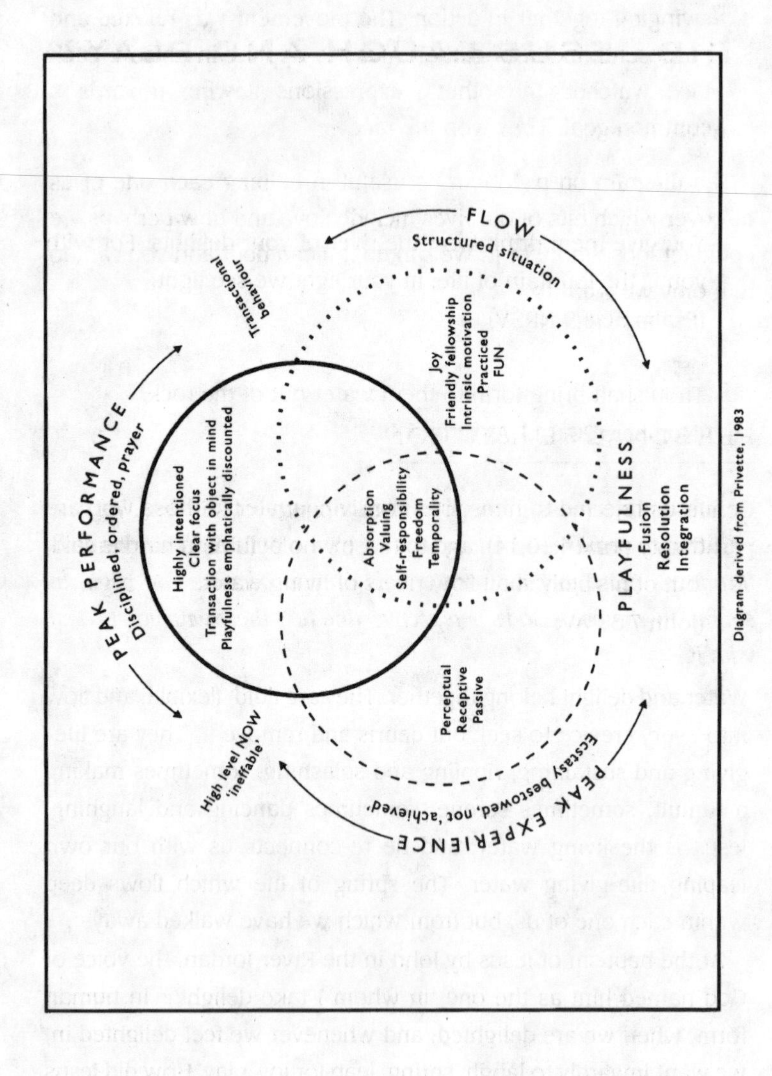

Diagram derived from Privette, 1983

6

DID JESUS LAUGH AND PLAY?

> You give them drink from the river of your delights. For with you is the fountain of life; in your light we see light.
> (Psalm 36:8,9 NRSV)
>
> Thou shalt bring forth to them water out of the rock.
> (Numbers 20:8,11 AV)[1]
>
> Jesus referred to himself as the living water to those who are thirsty (John 4:10,14), and to those who believe in him he said, 'out of his belly shall flow rivers of living water'.
> (John 7:38 AV)

Water and delight belong together. They are fluid, flexible, and flow into every crevice to seek out debris and remove it. They are life-giving and sustaining; rippling and splashing, sometimes making a tumult, sometimes serene, sometimes dancing and laughing. Jesus *is* the living water; and he re-connects us with our own leaping, life-giving water. The spring of life which flows deep within each one of us, but from which we have walked away.

At the baptism of Jesus by John in the River Jordan, the voice of God named him as the one 'in whom I take delight'.[2] In human form, when we are delighted, and whenever we feel delighted in, we want inwardly to laugh, spring, leap for joy, play. How did Jesus feel, as a person who was both delighting and delighted in? We have already seen how important childlikeness was to him, now it's time to take the image a little further.

THE CHURCH AND THE IMAGE OF JESUS LAUGHING

We have to admit it: there is a strong reluctance among many 'religious' people to visualise Jesus laughing. We have no classical art that depicts him at play or in the throes of belly-laughter, and this is a lack stemming from our cultural history.[3] In medieval times the way to celebrate fun and good humour was to attend the 'Festival of Fools'. Jesters and acrobats and clowns would fill the churches, the naves were crowded and laughter rolled down the aisles. It wasn't long before clerics felt it was all getting a bit out of hand, and so their leaders put a ban on any frivolity in church. Time passed, but it remained a religious conviction that people needed to be occupied in order to keep them out of mischief: leisure led to immorality. The 'people' were kept at work for hours on end to prevent them from getting into trouble. **Play** was seen to be about wantonness and luxury, it had no place in clean living. The landed gentry, of course, could be relied on to pursue idleness with candour and impunity. Indeed the pursuit of idleness became a sophisticated and even admired pastime. The upper classes, it was generally held, knew how to handle leisure, whereas the multitudes must be kept from it at all costs. A bit later on the system of beliefs that came to be known as the Protestant work ethic developed, and it was outlandish to suggest that Jesus might have been touched by jocularity. Images of Jesus laughing or playing were strictly out of bounds.

The result was an estrangement from our real selves, from the God-made image which springs up in each of us, the bit which is about delighting in God our Creator and receiving his delight in us. This loss is so great we are in danger of drying up from the inside.

HOW JESUS USED PLAYFULNESS

Jesus knew that putting energy to work and recouping it had to go hand in hand. The spending and giving out of self has to be

followed by a time of recovery, of resting, of playing. At the end of a long hard day, can't you imagine him taking time out to gambol with the village children? Enjoying their squeals of laughter as he danced with a toddler around his shoulders? There were other ways that he restored his soul too. Time after time in the story of his life it is recorded that 'he went away and hid from the people.'[4] We can only sense how he used those spaces, there are no black and white records. Yet the experience of regularly letting go and re-establishing delight with his Father – and with his disciples – overflowed into his ministry in remarkable ways.

For instance: there are four qualities of playfulness which undergird the ways in which Jesus taught. He wanted to so embody the love of God that men and women would yearn to be part of it. He did it like this:

1. Jesus would throw out sound-bite witticisms to catch the attention of those around him. He made use of extravagant exaggerations that were unerringly memorable. The rhetorical tradition of those days was to communicate in hyperbole – a form of overstatement that made a point – but Jesus would clothe his statements in ridiculousness. In literal fact, whoever saw a man with a wooden beam resting in his eye? Or a blind man left to lead another blind person? Or an overloaded camel trying to get through the eye of a needle?[5] Or someone wishing to shift a perfectly happy mulberry tree into the middle of the ocean? The very nonsensicality of such pictures seals them onto the mind's eye and makes sure their memory will return – with a chuckle. Jesus constantly used this ruse: to introduce a new idea he would dress it up as being preposterous. Whoever shifted a mountain by using a grain of mustard? Over the tumultuous years of the evangelists' lives, and down the centuries since then, these ridiculous juxtapositions of opposites *have been remembered*. The laugh they raised at the time and their instant good cheer have carried the

message far more effectively than any solemn pronouncement. Jesus was a fisher of men, and his bait was often wrapped around in laughter. But since then his sayings have been so reverentially examined that we have become immune to their spontaneity and originality.

2. Jesus was open to the wit and imagination of others. On one occasion, when he was hard-pressed and trying to avoid the demands of the crowds, his privacy was invaded by a woman who was a foreigner, a Syro-Phoenician. She asked him for help but, aware of his own exhaustion, he implied that his energies were reserved for the people of Israel. The children who are heirs should get the first bite of the cake, as it were, rather than the family pets. 'Ah,' replied the persistent and desperate woman, 'don't the dogs under the table get scraps dropped by the children? Even beggars get scraps from the master's table.' Jesus was so moved by her imaginative response that he gave her what she most craved.[6] Similar word-play is used concerning the description of the Samaritan woman's 'husband'. He enjoyed using sharply pointed verbal play when he duelled with the Pharisees who were trying to catch him out. He always won in the game of wit.

3. Jesus was a very popular guest. Women who were branded as immoral, tax-collectors who were hated, and publicans who were despised, all welcomed his company. He would hardly have been invited to their houses and their meals if he had been constantly solemn and retiring. Few people appreciate a good laugh and true playfulness more than those who are shunned, those from whom people habitually recoil. Yet it was these people on the edge of acceptable society with whom Jesus chose to spend time.

4. Perhaps most moving and profound of all is the way Jesus sometimes dealt with situations that called for rebuff. There are a few occasions where, when the text is read 'straight', it becomes

really difficult to credit the degree of rebuttal that is recorded. Many of these incidents involve Peter, the most ungrown-up disciple. Take a second look at the following:

- Peter's enthusiasm when he attempted to follow Jesus' example and walk on the water to meet him. 'Lord,' he cried as he sank, 'save me!' And Jesus replied, 'You have so little faith, why did you doubt?' (Matthew 14:29–31 NJB)[7]
- Peter's unconsidered exclamation, 'Never! You shall never wash my feet'. And Jesus replies, 'If I do not wash you, you can have no share with me.' (John 13:8 NJB)
- Peter's impetuous, 'I will lay down my life for you.' And Jesus' answer, 'Lay down your life for me? In all truth I tell you, before the cock crows you will have disowned me three times.' (John 13:37–8 NJB)[8]
- Clopas and his companion, desperate, disillusioned and bereaved, on their way out of Jerusalem and away from the collapse of all their deepest longings are met by someone they don't recognise. Jesus replies, 'O fools, and slow of heart . . .' (Luke 24:25 AV)

  Is it likely that just at the moment when his mission has been totally completed, and he is filled with the glory of the resurrection, that Jesus would choose to reprimand those who were despairing in such a way?

Is there another way of reading these passages? Could it be that Jesus was *chortling*[9] – that wonderful portmanteau word invented by Lewis Carroll which is a cross between a chuckle and a snort? Wouldn't his welcoming love rather say, 'You chumps! Look at it this way . . .'

In all the above instances, it seems inevitable that the profound and unconditional love of Jesus would be expressed by clothing his rebuke in a *tease*.[10] But a tease itself is ambivalent: it can take the form of a sneer, and make the one it is aimed at feel put down, or it can be affectionate and playful, and make the one who receives it feel stronger. Which manner do you imagine Jesus chose?

It is useful to remember that in medieval terms the word 'silly' was a form of endearment, of fondness and tolerance. Dame Julian says, 'God wills that a silly soul comes to him plainly, nakedly, homely, for he wishes to solace and mirth his dearworthy friends.' And the word 'fool' referred to a clown or court jester, someone who was a windbag[11] and incited belly laughter, who was held in great affection by the general public.

There are other significant instances where the humour of Jesus was barely submerged. Take another look at these:

- When Jesus appeared totally unexpectedly to his closest friends, those who thought his mission had failed and his life was over, in their shock they heard him say, 'a ghost has no flesh and bones as you can see I have . . . Have you got anything to eat?' (Luke 24:40–3 JB)
- And later on, when his friends were wondering about their own future, Jesus chuckles, 'If I want John to stay behind until I come, what does it matter to you?' (John 21:22 JB)
- Or again, just before he goes back to be with his Father, isn't there a good-humoured tease in his reply: 'It is not for you to know the times or dates that the Father has decided!' (Acts 1:7 JB)

All these remarks were made to people who were troubled and uneasy: the all-encompassing compassion of Jesus must have gentled the potential reproof with laughter.

OUR RESPONSE

That love that won't give up, that waits with arms spread wide and playfully teases us for our own self-impotence, out of our self-importance, is insistent; maybe we shall find that under its softening influence we become more open to his love and power and purpose than when we doggedly insist on keeping our sinfulness up front.

I am gathering this chapter together on Good Friday. Words like betrayal, denial, separation, isolation, sin, are rebounding in every church and chapel. It is natural that things get leaden, weighted, introverted, spiralling downwards. If we dare to, we can face changing that. Some of the judgemental forces we hold – and even encourage – in our imaginations can be redeemed in the light of the unconditional love, the love that delights in us, of our Father. We have a need to stay with our attitudes of shock and horror at the passion story we have inherited. But if we can sometimes let it go, or loosen some of the emphasis on self-introspection, we can allow in a picture of Jesus who was assured, assuring, and at appropriate moments playfully encouraging.[12]

In the course of four chapters, St John puts together the final thoughts and deepest expressions of love that Jesus most wanted his friends to remember. Five times during this long conversation Jesus says, 'Ask God in my name'. That is, he tells us to ask God in the character and desire of Jesus, in the way he expressed his love towards God and us. And then, as a final act of supreme confidence and generosity before he went out into the dark to face the worst experience that this world could hurl at him, at that very instant of grief and bewilderment, he bequeathed us his – **joy**. Jesus said, 'I speak these things in the world so that they may have **my joy made complete in themselves**' (John 17:13 NRSV).

If Jesus played, teased, gave, joked, even as he loved and prayed, can't we?

PERSONAL REFLECTION

It is said of Samuel Johnson (eighteenth century) that he exclaimed, 'This merriment of parsons is mighty offensive!' Is there something in me that still holds to this view? Do I somehow feel threatened by the idea of putting holiness and playfulness together??

*

> Dear God, I know the task I did for you yesterday had great holes in it, but please take it in Jesus' name. I don't have to wait until what I offer is perfect, for it to be acceptable and fully fit, before I give it to you. You know how I fail, but you have also told me you delight in each one of us even though we are fools. Let your living water wash over me forgiving, cleansing and delighting. Foolishness in others never deterred Jesus from loving them, with playfulness; may my foolishness not deter me from offering myself to you, and, when it is appropriate, offering playfulness to others. In your name only I ask it.

7

GOD AND PLAYFULNESS

Proverbs: Of the creation, Wisdom says:
'Then was I at his [the Creator's] side each day,
His darling and delight, playing in his presence
continually,
Playing over his whole world,
When he made earth's foundations firm.'
(8:30, 31, 29 REB)

Ezekiel: 'I myself shall tend my flock' says the Lord God,
'I shall search for the lost . . . give my flock their
proper food,
and leave the healthy and strong to play.'
(34:15, 16 REB)

Zechariah: 'Now,' says the Lord, 'I shall come back to Zion, and Jerusalem will be called the City of Faithfulness. I will rescue my people. The streets of the city will be full of boys and girls at play. They will be my people, and I shall be their God.' (8:3, 7, 5, 8 REB)

2 Corinthians: I will welcome you and be your father, and you shall be my sons and daughters, says the Almighty Lord.
(6:8 JB)

The word 'God' goes side by side with light, delight, enlightening,

lightening the weight; it goes with rejoicing, exulting, thanking, praising; for some it carries ecstasy and exaltation. There are also words like justice and righteousness and judgement, but these heavy words are discussed more frequently in other books, and used more often in sermons – those ones that constantly exhort us to do better. For this chapter lets stay with the Light, and the One who created it, and who created us, as we are.

God the Creator designed the world we live in, however much we have misused it. We know that nature is red in tooth and claw, and that every animal and bird and fish depends for its existence on the destruction of members of other species; we know that

> Small bugs have big bugs upon their backs to bite 'em,
> and big bugs have bigger bugs and so ad infinitum . . .

The natural world, as we find it today, seems to depend on a process of one part thriving by feeding off another. We know too well how much this system can encroach on us, as humans, and on the way we treat each other. But we also know that each unit of creation is unique and individual, and God's delight in his creation is all about that uniqueness. John Taylor[1] points out, it is the bee-ness of the bee that delights God; it is when the tiger is being at its most tiger-ish that God is glorified; it is the high jump of the flea and the speed of the dragonflies' wings that makes him hoot for joy.[2]

Michael Mayne writes, 'it is the separate integrity of each thing on earth that delights us, the fact that a snail is a snail and not a beetle',[3] and he notes the childlikeness of this peculiar thrill. As Tom Wright describes it, it is when penguins are sliding over the ice and clouds are dancing across the sky that they are being themselves to the glory of God. He continues:

> The people of God, knowing him as Creator, understand that

> as such he is a God full of extraordinary ideas and inventive imagination. We just have to think for two minutes about the world of creation and imagine the same God creating a giraffe and creating a strawberry, the same God creating a waterfall and creating a new-born baby's face. Human beings are designed to . . . draw out the praises of creation, understand them, and lay them before the throne of God in *gladness*.[4]

The secular psychologist Aric Sigman insists that: 'Popeye's ability to state most confidently "I am what I am what I am what I am" is a *gift*.'

Our God is the author of joy, delight, gladness, playfulness; more, he has created the world in such a way that, if only we pause to watch the clouds scampering, the snowflakes dancing, the fireflies chasing, the leopard cubs teasing, the leaves of autumn scattering, he can be *seen* to be playful. His playfulness is in the breezes[5] and the shadows, the waves and angelfish and the hermit crabs. Add to those things, the extraordinary fact that God is prepared to produce acres and acres, miles upon miles, of wild flowers blooming unseen, of white water splashing unheard, of hyaenas and kookaburras and mocking birds laughing unremarked; the patterns and colour and movement and vitality preposterously going nowhere for 'no one's' benefit, and his playfulness is undoubtable. He positively designs things that show off his playfulness, but for the most part we choose not to notice. We prefer being 'grown up'.

'Grown-upness' can lead us into strange places. Here's another story:

> Once upon a time there was a small child – about seven years old – who sat at her desk feeling lonely and confused. She was at the back of the class and she couldn't tell what the teacher was on about. The other children at her boarding school (high

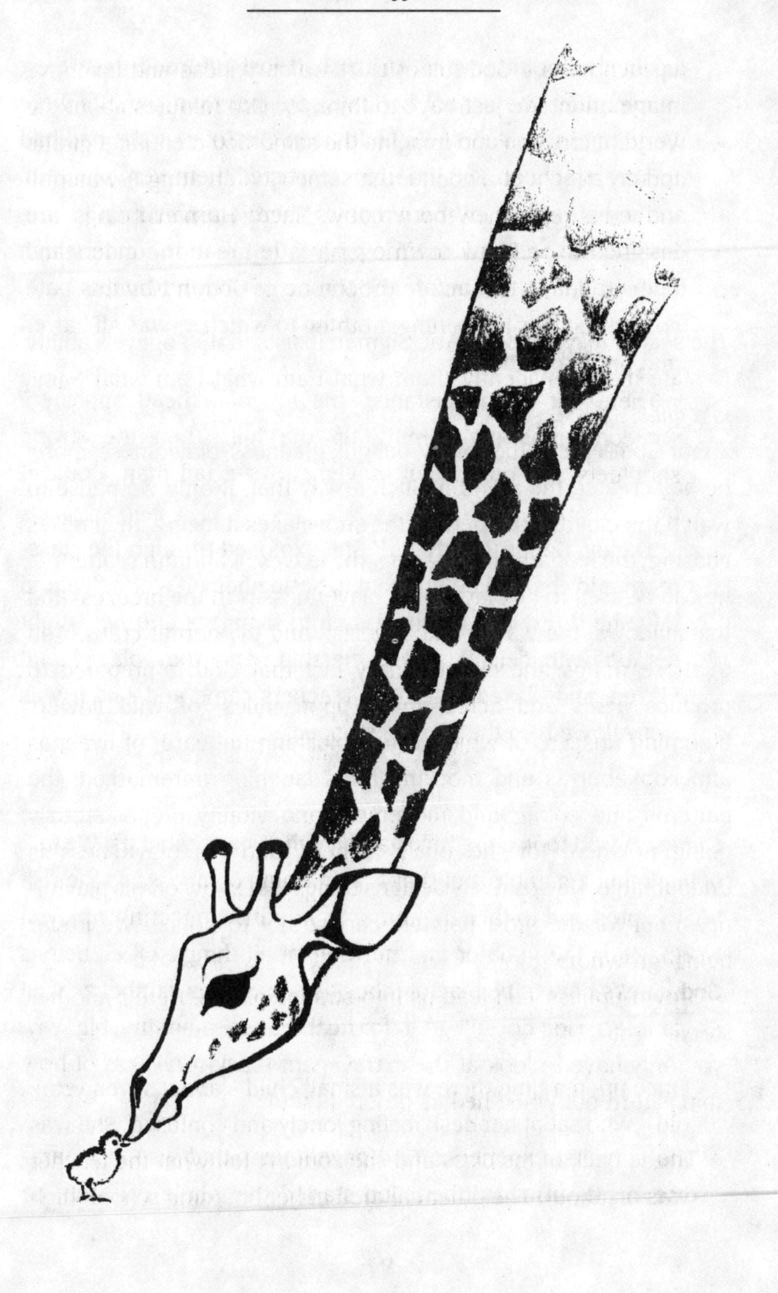

up in the mountains of Africa) had just returned from their homes after the school holidays; but her own parents were Very Important People and had been On Tour so she had had to stay at school. The little girl Respected them Very Much.

She looked out of the window. There wasn't much to see. The school path led down over a little hill to the gate which opened onto a side road. Nobody came or went by that gate, so nothing was happening, nothing to watch. It was all barren and pretty pointless.

Then, out of the distance, the top of a head appeared: someone must be coming up the hill. Then the strong shoulders and purposeful movement of a tall man. Could it be . . .?

'Daddy, Daddy, Daddy . . .!' She exploded through the classroom and charged down the hill, beside herself with relief and joy. She threw her whole body into his arms and he caught her up with delight and ownership. And they played and played, and played. Then the Teachers came and said it was Not Allowed, so the playing stopped.

*

Our great God took a massive gamble when he created us. We talk of life being a gamble, but that is as nothing compared to the risk he was prepared to take in putting us into his staggeringly playful world. He is the initiator and nurturer of all things. Of all beings God knows how to be playful (does he sometimes gambol as well as gamble?). God doesn't go in for neat management in a big way: you only have to look at the extravagant topsy-turvyness of how things turn out when he has ordered them:

- The very first experience God gave humankind was in a paradise, a playground. When God started the whole caboosh, he played hide-and-seek in a garden. It was only as we shouldered free will that work came upon the scene, and the Garden of Eden was barred.

- Then he asked Moses to lead the people he had chosen to love into a wild place with no water, no shelter and no food.
- He told Gideon to face up to ten thousand armed warriors using a mere hundred men holding trumpets.
- He asked David, the runt of his family who was turned out to shepherd the sheep in the hills, to be the king of his people.
- He selected Amos, a picker of figs, to be among the highest politicians in the land and sting the nation into social action.
- He confounded an old man, Zechariah, by telling him to impregnate his equally old wife, and then made him dumb because he had doubted his ability to do so. Eventually, the baby that resulted from this unlikely union grew up to be a great prophet.
- He chose a simple girl from an insignificant village to bear and bring up his Son.
- Supremely, God chose to get the world back into line by incarnating himself, pitting himself against the risks and trials of the world, and embodying love in this one and only Son. Having exposed himself to unimaginable insults and suffering, he then proceeded to offer abundant life with him in his presence forever.

Great Creator God: God of design that spoofs all our preconceived notions of order, may I be alongside you in your playing today.

We, as managers of our own lives, prefer order, and control, and containment.

GOD CAN MAKE IT ALL UP!

It's such a strange phrase – 'make up'. It can refer to

- the act of creating, inventing, making something out of nothing
- making up a story – good, bad, fictional, metaphorical, mysterious
- the art of forgiving and being forgiven
- the ritual of putting my best face on
- and the extension of this, the elaborate craft of turning a human face into the stylised one of a clown, a jester, or a fool

The professional fool is an expert. His foolishness may be way above our wisdom. The fool sees things and keeps quiet, but turns them into comedy we can all understand. The fool, male or female, is master of the skills of unpredictability that mirror those of God.

(***Holy and extravagant unleashed Spirit: enable me to leap and dance and let go with you as you exuberantly unleash chains today***.)

God is 'playing' with us:

- When the burdens we carry are heavy, and our yoke irks us, God lightens them. As Jesus the carpenter eased the yoke to fit each animal, he eases the weights to fit our own shoulders. But we have to trust in his playing with them, if it is going to work.
- When to us the path seems dark and muddy and unknown, God the Holy Spirit lights it up. But we have to see the play of light and shadow, if it is to be understood.
- When we are bowed down with responsibility, God the Creator lets us in to some of his delight. But we have to be open to it, if his playfulness is to get us through.

Our triune God will show us his abundant playfulness with joy. But there can be no hanging back or holding on: he wants us to abandon ourselves to him. Our God is a rumbustious God; he does not ask us to be staid, but to join in with him as he creates, out of topsy-turveyness, whatever it is that is in keeping with his purpose, his Kingdom, his peace.

PERSONAL REFLECTION

It has such a dramatic effect on my relationship with God if I can throw up all the things I can't make sense of, all the *non-sense* things, and leave them for him to catch, leave them in his hands. He can deal with them. It's my own pomposity in keeping them close to myself that stifles me.

Lord,
I know you are always with me, all the time and everywhere;
but I am not always with you.
You can see and understand all the obstructions and interferences and curtains that get in the way better than I can.
Help me not to lose my way or become too discouraged. Show me how to deal with them; and to know that you are always there, whether I can see you or not.
When I am heavy, lead me to remember your playfulness.

8

PLAYFULNESS IN *ME*?

Girls and boys come out to play,
  the moon doth shine as bright as day!
Leave your supper and leave your sleep,
  and join your playfellows in the street.

Come with a whoop and come with a call,[1]
  come with goodwill or not at all.
Up the ladder and down the wall,
  a halfpenny loaf will do for all.

Perhaps this nursery rhyme grew out of a folk memory of the words in Zechariah that head the previous chapter. Wherever it comes from, it does pose strange priorities. 'Leave your supper and leave your sleep . . .' just in order to play? That seems inappropriate today. But bearing in mind the long hours of child labour which existed when this rhyme started, it points to the strong desire for play, in whatever circumstances.

There are important values to take note of here: they are about

- making the most of any opportunity;
- the trigger of an *invitation*;
- moving together with a single purpose;
- making provision for everybody; in this verse there is no hierarchy or sense of competition;

– and the attraction of excitement and adventure, perhaps even risk.

All these things apply to playfulness in prayer. Do *I* apply them in *my* prayer, and the group I pray with?

*

Have you forgotten how to play? I have. I know how to work, to be busy, to care for others, to be still, to work with my computer (a bit!) – but to play? As a mother I played with my children – but they are grown now. As a lover I played with my love – but maturity tends to invite 'dignity'. Could I therefore ever allow myself to play **with God?** Can I let my hair down with God? Can I jest with God? I can fight with God; I can be silent with God; I can joy in God; but can I laugh with God?

The end of a children's book puts it like this:

> And snakes and bats and all those others
> That only God loves – or mothers –
> How could God think up all those things?
> The different songs that each bird sings,
> the cockatoo and crocodile –
> I think they must have made God smile.
> It must have been the way he played.
> And when at last that all were made,
> From tiny gnat to tall giraffe –
> I wish I could have heard God laugh![2]

WHY CAN'T I?

So what stops me from hearing that rolling, creative, inviting, contagious, upholding laughter?

What holds me back, and intimidates me? Is it something to do with allowing my precious self-image to melt, and opening myself up to *intimacy*?

And what makes me so fearful of intimacy? Is it to do with shedding my self-protection? Can I face dismantling the scaffold of roles and status that hold me up? Maybe I might even suspect I could be *made to look a fool*, and what could be worse than that?

If, like the hermit crab, I can dare to come out of my shell, even while I am scuttling across the sand to find another shell to house me, in my bareness I might meet the One who loves me, and whom I love. And I might find that intimacy that is unique between me and the One who made me. Intimacy and playfulness are very closely connected.

PLAYFULNESS

Playfulness is about abandoning my own concerns into the inventiveness and unexpectedness of another. It's the ultimate **let-go**:

letting go my self-imposed pompousness;
letting go my disguised self-pity;
letting go of my need to worry and be anxious;
letting go my have-tos, my ought-tos, and musts;
letting go of my earnestness, my 'worthiness', my trying-hard;
letting go of childishness, look-at-me-ness, tantrums at not-getting-what-I-want;
getting free from the relentless tirade of self-criticism.

As Richard Holloway says, it is 'the real faith of the Christian that is more like a rolling jazz session than a march on the barrack square.'[3]

All this can be undeniably difficult: there has been so much in my education about gaining control, and particularly self-control. About not letting on where it hurts, keeping cool in a crisis, and – being British – about keeping the lid down even when I am exultant.

Yet Harry Williams writes that it is only when I am able to

> laugh at myself that I accept myself, and when I laugh at other people in genuine mirth that I accept them. Self-acceptance in laughter is the very opposite of self-accusation or pride. For in the laughter I accept myself not because I'm some sort of super-person, but precisely because I'm not. There is nothing funny about a super-person. There is everything funny about a man who thinks he is.
>
> In laughing at my own claims to importance or regard I receive myself in a sort of loving forgiveness which is an echo of God's forgiveness of me. In much conventional contrition there is a selfishness and pride which are scarcely hidden. In our desperate self-concern we blame ourselves for not being the super-person we think we really are. But in laughter we sit light to ourselves. That is why laughter is the purest form of our response to God. . . . For to sit light to yourself is true humility. Pride cannot rise to levity.[4]

LETTING-GO – INTO GOD

It's quite simple: playfulness is the antidote to taking myself too seriously. When I feel the approach of that morass of self-decomposition, that threat of being sucked under in the mire of my own insufficiency and ineptitude and blockages (which is in fact the awareness of the sin of the world of which I am a part), it is in turning to the playfulness of the Christ-child that I am retrieved from moroseness. The indulgent depression of self-castigation is never modelled in the Good News.[5] It is only as I strip myself of my pretensions that the bit of the image of God that is in me is uncovered. Whether that bit of his image in me becomes tarnished over the years, or scarred, or distorted or dented, the Creator *still* delights in it, *still* wants it to respond by receiving and sharing this delight.

THE ART OF THE FOOL

The medieval court jester could say things, and spell out truths, that were disallowed and denied in normal conversation; clowns

who appear clumsy and awkward and childlike can get away with social protests and ridiculous propositions that we don't ordinarily want to look at. The clown undercuts our so-called intellectualism, and shows up our pomposity for what it is. The clown reveals the preposterous expectations that I cling on to, and allows them to melt away. St Paul claimed that he was a fool for the sake of Jesus Christ,[6] and he would heartily endorse the modern clown ministry headed up by Roly Bain.[7] 'Holy Fools' live out the vulnerability and openness that enable us to glimpse new truth about ourselves and God.

PRAYER

Roly Bain insists that holiness and humour go hand in hand. It's about being true to the unique self, and yet not taking it too seriously. To know yourself and yet laugh at yourself. To be able to open up to the daringly unpredictable, and not mind too much how often you get things wrong. That is why children with their insatiable questioning and their unguarded loving give adults the licence to play. He has written: 'Prayer is to be lived and revelled in, rather than said "nicely". Maybe too often we end up saying our prayers rather than praying, clinging to the wreckage of dull custom rather than sailing off into uncharted waters.'[8]

Abandoned prayer is marked by its sense of expectancy, readiness for anything, comic, routine, or tragic, but it is without any sort of demand. Real prayer doesn't even assume preferential treatment. It doesn't state its preferred objectives. It says, 'I don't know what is in store for me, but whatever it is I know you will stay beside me as long as I stay beside you.' He continues:

The prayer of the vulnerable lover is not a shopping list or a news bulletin or choice titbits of half-baked theology or moralistic judgements.

The prayer of the vulnerable lover leaves everything in God's hands, starts from scratch, and offers 'Here am I! Send me!'

The prayer of the vulnerable lover has no strings attached, no limits to its intention, and no advice to proffer.

The prayer of the vulnerable lover derives from a willingness to play, a longing for the Kingdom. And a simple love of God.[9]

GOD LAUGHING

There are rare occasions when people are given a profound glimpse into the glory and closeness of God laughing. Sometimes an experience is given that infects everything else experienced in life thereafter. One such incident, reported by a woman who was on retreat, occurred while she was walking in the woods in silence. She heard, 'Sit on my shoulder as a young child does, and I will show you wonders you have never conceived.' Jesus carried her as he and she went through his whole life, laughing and laughing; and even in his passion there was submerged laughter in the strength of his confidence and hope. It changed her entire perspective of God for the rest of her life. A similar experience came from a priest working in a down-town area. He described it in personal correspondence. During an individually guided retreat, this man meditated upon the question Jesus put to the blind man (Luke 18:35–43). 'What is it that you want me to do for you?' He dared to reply, and his prayer was answered. He writes:

> Wow!! Joy!! Laughter!!!! – and he LAUGHED, LAUGHED uncontrollably, to such an extent he literally fell over with

laughter! He experienced what Irenaeus meant: 'the glory of God is a person fully alive'. *This must have been how the woman with the haemorrhage felt when she was made whole! Cartwheeling for joy everywhere – 'rejoicing with unutterable and exalted joy' (Peter 1:8). And I caught a glimpse of Heaven! Alleluia!!*

His life and prayer were changed. There was exuberance and exaltation all rolled into one.

THE MAGNITUDE OF GOD

In playfulness, I can sometimes break through the barriers of magnitude and awe that separate me from God. For instance, look at this:

God is great and unknowable.
His knowledge and wisdom are unfathomable, unapproachable, a vast distance away from our puny understanding.
Think of the grains of sand on just one beach. In imagination, build a cube of sand one foot long, one foot wide, and one foot high. Imagine the number of grains of sand in that one cube.
Make the sandcastle one yard by one yard by one yard. It's very big; there are multitudes of grains of sand in that castle, unimaginable numbers. Let your mind wander over all those granules.
Extend the castle to *five* yards by five yards by five yards. What sense can be made of numbers now?
Think of *one unique* grain of sand in the bottom left-hand corner.

That *one grain* represents Earth, a star in one universe that God has created.[10]
And that God loves me.

Now that is something to laugh about.

PERSONAL REFLECTION

- To arrive at that place where I can get lost in wonder, love, praise and play, I have to feel safe. Lion cubs, puppies, young children only play where it is *safe*. Am I safe with God? Or is he still a judgemental Father to me, and do I still have to cringe before him? He has said he wants to call me 'friend';[11] do I insist on still being a slave?
- He so often laughs back at me in my prayers – when I get it incongruously wrong and he lets me know that *he* knows it all, I don't. When I get too bumptious by half – he gives me an appropriate put-down, just as he did to Peter when he was too impetuous.
- At those times when I get too big for my boots, thinking my way is so much better than the way of the person I'm not getting on with, God reminds me that he loves that one quite as much as he loves me, and he chuckles about it.
- The only possible response is that of the loved child: to respond incredulous with playfulness, thankfulness, and abandonment into the arms of God. And then *I know* that

  if I fail, God still loves me;
  if I get the wrong end of the stick, God will still love me;
  if I make a hash of things, God still goes on loving me;
  (maybe I will feel it is more difficult to hear his voice, I have

stepped backwards, but God continues to love me, because he can't help it, he *is* Love)
if I turn away from him, he continues to love me;
if I fail to own him, or even deliberately betray him, God will continue to love me;
(maybe others will find it difficult to see God's light in me, but it is me that will have hidden it)
if I remain unhealed, God loves me even more;
when I am wounded, vulnerable, receptive, his love has no bounds because it is unfettered by my competence.

Praise to him in everything.

Every time I want to leap and dance in his presence – he will leap and dance with me; holding me, holding on to me, releasing and catching me, twirling me with an exchange of freedom and intimacy, closeness and letting go. Safety and risk rolled into one; assurance and challenge mixing and twisting. I am leaping into his welcome.

9

PLAYING AMONG THE MYSTICS

Come, Mary's Son, my Friend; our Fullness is in You.[1]

This 'fullness' naturally includes play-fullness. A very young baby plays by itself. When it is fed, safe, comfortable and warm we can watch and marvel at such an amazing ability to be self-sufficient; gurgling and playing with toes and fingers and voice the baby will be totally absorbed and content. But as we grow up we discover we need an invitation to be playful. Where can we find the grounds for that invitation?

THE MODEL OF THE 'MYSTICS'

In our imagination, we seldom see the writers who have left us their deepest spiritual insights as wanting to play. Those revered people, with their raptures, visions, and their other-worldliness, were they open to *fun?* They were engrossed in things that are eternal and non-material; was carefreeness part of their experience? Think of the holiest people you know, those most genuinely sanctified; isn't it their quick and bubbling laughter that comes to mind? Their sense of fun and mischief; their resistance to being taken seriously as individuals? People like this who have been most often in the modern public eye would include Michael Ramsey, Michael Hollings, Mother Teresa. It's almost as if they have some secret knowledge, some access to mystery and mystical properties that escape us ordinary people. They point to the closeness of the sublime with the ridiculous.

This chapter is made up of selected quotations from some of the writings of past centuries which have been most loved down the ages. Some of the earliest texts in the Old Testament have been noted in other chapters; here, Celtic Christians are our starting point.

✤ Early Christian 'Croons'. The Celtic followers of Christ were constantly aware of the presence of God in their daily tasks. Life for them was tough, lonely, monotonous, and often dangerous; they smoothed these hard conditions by 'crooning' as they worked. They surprise us by binding together paradox and play. These are some examples:

(i) while caring for the cow:

> Ho my little cow, ho my brown cow!
>   Ho my little cow, ho my brown cow!
> Little cow of my heart, dear, beloved,
>   Jewel of the white cows art thou.
> My little brindled cow, dear, beloved,
>   Safe thou wouldst cross the crest of the peaks.
> My sweet little cow, dear, beloved,
>   With me thou wouldst cross the crest of the waves.
> Ho my little cow, ho my brown cow!

(ii) or while milking:

> Bless, O God, my little cow,
> And the milking of my hands, O God.
> Bless, O God, each teat,
> Bless, O God, each finger;
> Bless Thou each drop
> That goes into my pitcher, O God!

(iii) or at the end of weaving a piece of cloth, perhaps as a gift for a son:

This is no second-hand cloth,
And it is not begged,
It is not property of cleric,
But thine own property,
O son of my body.
By moon and by sun,
In the presence of God,
Keep thou it!
Mayest thou enjoy it,
Mayest thou wear it,
Mayest thou finish it,
Until thou find it
In shreds,
In strips,
In rags,
In tatters!

✤ During the eleventh to thirteenth centuries there grew a particular sort of mysticism among holy women living in the Rhineland. One of these, ***Mechthilde of Magdeburg*** suffered greatly both physically and spiritually, but her burning love for God grew from one intensity to another. Her writings are forthright and earthy. She says: 'I am constrained to follow God naked, barefoot and stripped of earthly things.' None the less she states, 'A prior is to cheer the sick, even to be merry and laugh with them in a godly manner.' ***For God wants us for his playmates***. Her idea of heaven is where

> All the Blest, filled and enchanted, sing for joy, and laugh and leap in ordered dance. They flow and swim and fly and climb, from tiered choir to choir still upward.[2]

- Later on in the Middle Ages, ***Meister Eckhart*** expresses playfulness like this:

Do you want to know what goes on in the core of the Trinity?

I will tell you:
In the core of the Trinity the Father laughs –
and gives birth to the Son;
The Son laughs back at the Father –
and gives birth to the Spirit;
The whole Trinity laughs –
and gives birth to us.[3]

Then there was ***St Francis***, with his troubadours and '*joculatores*':

> St Francis had no 'ifs' and 'buts' about God's love. He was totally taken up and light-headed with the joy of it. He taught people to throw away their self-concern, and approach God with simplicity and childlikeness, revelling in prayer. Those who followed him became known as God's minstrels and jesters. Ordinary careworn people would flock to be with them, to join in the exhilaration and freedom of this sort of merriment, the awareness of God's outpouring love. If people were awkward or naive or ignorant it made no difference, they were still *loved*. One friar who did not know Latin felt he could not attend Mass, so he decided to do what he was best at doing, and he did it in honour of the Virgin Mary. He cartwheeled for her! She was so pleased by this offering she sent him the gift of levitation, and he cartwheeled right up to the ceiling.[4]
>
> The orders founded by St Francis emphasised poverty, but they were reknowned for their singing, joking and merrymaking.[5]

✤ A bit later, ***Dame Julian of Norwich*** makes 'merriment' one of her main themes:

> Then I saw our Lord royally reign in his house, full-filling it with joy and mirth, himself endlessly to gladden and solace his dearworthy friends, full homely and full courteously, with marvellous melody of endless love. . . . We are his bliss; in us he liketh without end. And thus he willeth merrily that our soul be occupied.
>
> It is God's will . . . that we seek him wilfully, gladly and merrily, without unskilful heaviness and vain sorrow. And then sheweth our courteous Lord himself to the soul – well merrily and with glad cheer – with friendly welcoming. Full glad and merry is our Lord of our prayer . . . for wrath and friendship be two contraries. It is the most worship to him of anything that we may do, that (in our penance), we live gladly and merrily for his love.[6]

When she is ill and at a point of death, she sees the Fiend near her with his horrible stench and fearsome expression. 'For this sight I laughed merrily, and that made them to laugh that were about me, and their laughing was a liking to me.' She gets rid of him by laughing. This is an extraordinarily moving account, given in chapter 13 of her *Revelations of Divine Love*.

✤ Another contemporary book is ***The Cloud of Unknowing***[7] by an unknown author.

> Give attention to the marvellous way it works within your soul. It is a sudden and unheralded impulse speedily springing up to God like a spark from a coal, and it is marvellous the number of impulses that can be formed. It is far away from any delusion, false imagination or fanciful opinion. . . . Wonderful delights and comforts come from within, rising and springing

> up from the abundance of spiritual gladness . . . which are not to be held suspect. To be brief, I believe that anyone who has experienced them could not hold them suspect.
>
> Wait courteously and humbly the will of Our Lord, and do not snatch over-hastily like a greedy greyhound, however hungry you may be. Refrain from rough and great stirrings of your spirit. Perhaps you think that this is childishly and playfully spoken. But I believe that whoever has the grace to do and feel as I say would find himself having good playful fun with Him as a father does with a child, kissing and embracing, and happy he should be. [Other translations put it 'he should feel good gamesome play with Him'.]

With great common sense this author warns us about what is *not* to be mistaken for gamesomeness.

> Some have a fixed stare as if they were sheep affected by brain disease; some hang their heads on one side as if there were a worm in their ear; some cry and whine in their throats, so greedy and hasty are they to say what they think. Some twist their heads quaintly to one side, and up with their chins; they gape with their mouths as if they would hear with them [or as if they were catching flies, p. 87]. Some, when they come to speak, jab with their fingers their other hand, or their own breast or the breast of those they are talking to. Some can neither stand still nor sit still nor lie still unless they are wagging their feet or else doing something with their hands. Some row with their arms in time with their speaking, as if they had to swim over a great stretch of water. Some are continually smiling at every other word they say, as if they were silly japing jugglers misbehaving. A seemly demeanour brings with it a sober bearing and a cheerful attitude, without instability of heart and restlessness of mind.

In a letter the same author continues:

> It is quite sufficient for you that you feel yourself pleasantly stirred up – you know not what except that in this impulse you have no thought of anything less than God, and your will is simply directed towards God. . . . We love God, desire God, and finally rest with complete pleasure and full consent in God'.

And again in a letter the author writes:

> Say to your Lord, 'What I am I offer you, for it is You.' . . . The only thing that matters now is that the unseeing awareness of your bare blind being, be gladly borne up in the eager longing of love. . . . He will make you both joyously lissom and pleasantly pliant to that perfection . . . utterly stripped of yourself, your nakedness clothed in Him as He is.[8]

✤ In the sixteenth century ***St Ignatius Loyola*** implored his followers: 'Laugh, and grow strong!'

✤ In the early seventeenth century ***St Francis de Sales*** writes of something similar in a letter:

> Our enemy is a great clatterer, do not trouble yourself at all about him. He cannot hurt you. Mock at him and let him go on. Do not strive with him; ridicule him, for it is all nothing. He has howled round about all the saints, and made plenty of hubbub, but to what purpose? In spite of it all, there they are, seated in the place which he has already lost – the wretch![9]

✤ Later in the same century ***Thomas Traherne*** wrote *Centuries*,[10] a book that 'sweeps its readers free from the spiritual stagnation of this world's present dread'.[11] In it he states:

> Souls are God's jewels . . . God only being the Giver and I the Receiver. . . . He is not an Object of Terror, but Delight. He

> delighteth in our happiness more than we. . . . You may infinitely delight in God as your Father, Friend and Benefactor, and in yourself as His Heir, Child and Bride. . . . The end to which He guideth all this profitableness is to delight our senses, enflame us with His love, and make us amiable before Him, and delighters in His blessedness. He drowned our understanding in a multitude of wonders; transported us with delights, and enriched us with joys and pleasures. . . . For all things in Heaven and Earth attend upon us: we ought to answer and observe them. But God winketh at our defect, all the World attending us while we are about some little trifling business.[12]

Perhaps it is with this last point that we should pause. Do we, in our frenetically busy and stressful lives, give ourselves sufficient time and opportunity to take in all the blessings with which we are showered? Is that partly why we don't see God as being playful? Is that how we manage to block out his constant invitation to play with him? The mystics insist that they experience God in the smallest, everyday things. Do we?

Finally, ***St John Chrysostum***[13] hints at what can happen when playfulness is combined with tragedy. He paints a wonderful picture of Christ confronting the Devil himself. It concerns the 'harrowing' of hell. When Jesus the Christ went down into hell immediately after his death on the cross, he went there on his Father's business of freeing the souls that had been lost there. Does he plead with Satan? Curse him? Or simply *mock* him? Hell was abolished because the Devil was taunted with laughter: the gates were broken and those imprisoned let out simply because the Devil couldn't stand the mockery. It was the same when Dame Julian got rid of his hideous presence when he appeared at her supposed deathbed: she laughed at him. Evil cannot stand in the company of wholesome, rollicking laughter. It is dissolved and transformed as light melts darkness.

Many of the mystics make reference to the fact that we experience God as playing hide-and-seek with us: now you see him, now you don't. The apparent elusiveness of God is the subject of most

writers on mysticism. In a child, such a 'game' builds up delight and trust. As adults we would gain more from this experience if we were less afraid of it. God never wills to impose threat upon us; it is we who fail to keep our faith in playfulness robust and steady. Jesus said, 'Behold! I am with you always', but we can't always see him. Meister Eckhart reassures us: 'God never goes far off. He is always close at hand, and even if he cannot remain under your roof, still he goes no further away than outside the door, where he stands.'[14]

PERSONAL REFLECTION

'Come, Mary's Son, my Friend' is an invitation; 'our fullness is in You' is an affirmation, a desire to be part of its unfolding.

Do we need to **invite** God into our lives, and the lives of those we are praying for? Is God's presence and power realised to a greater extent by this invitation? The writings of the mystics seem to encourage us to be open as God invites us to be in that presence and power, to receive belovedness and delight. Maybe I can, myself, **invite** God more warmly and with a greater welcome into my living. Even, (dare I say it?) to be so unguarded as to invite his playfulness.

It is a great mistake to keep our prayer continuously solemn.
*It is about **trust**, and **childlikeness**, and **abandonment** to God.*

10

ALONGSIDE THE PAIN AND THE HURT

Behold, thou desireth truth in the inward parts: and in the hidden part thou shalt make me to know wisdom . . .

Make me to hear joy and gladness; that the bones which thou hast broken may rejoice.

Psalm 51:6, 8 (AV)

If thou hast no liking to meditate on My Passion with weeping eyes because of the bitter agony I suffered, then meditate on it with a laughing heart, because of the joyous benefit thou will find in it.

Henry Suso, a fourteenth-century mystic[1]

Poetry and Hums aren't things that you get, they're things that get you.

Pooh's Little Instruction Book[2]

PRECEDENTS

Lewis Carroll, Spike Milligan, Lionel Blue, Norman Cousins, Marti Caine, Michael Bentine, Tony Hancock, John Cleese, Brian Keenan and John McCarthy[3] are a varied collection of names, and there are many more that could be added to them. What is common to this selection is that they all declared publicly that they intended to get through their troubles – and these were varied enough – through the means of play and laughter.

These people affirm an extraordinary paradox: that tragedy can be borne more hopefully when playfulness is present.

In its turn, to be authentic and grounded, playfulness must be aware of tears. The way of a God-filled life is like a dual carriageway of pain and delight – but there are many cross-over points. It is a parallel path: to share with others our pain, and to share with others our delight. There are times to show how we hurt, and others to expand our joys, even the small ones. In this chapter we will look at whether pain can be touched by playfulness.

We have seen that Love needs love in return; we have seen that Delight needs to be delighted in; just so, suffering needs recognition and at some level it needs to be shared. But there is a basic difference; love and delight can be mutual, but the sharing of pain can only be partial. The one who is alongside the pain of another can genuinely 'feel for' the hurting, but only rarely can they dive to the same depths. Strangely enough, the bridge that links them is often a sort of playfulness. Here is a moving example of how this can happen.

In a recent book John Bayley describes the last illness of his wife, the philosopher and novelist Iris Murdoch. She had a particularly distressing form of Alzheimer's disease. Right through the book, his infinite and tender form of waiting-care never wavers. It is made all the more poignant because a near-playfulness keeps breaking through. Bayley is discussing how 'teasing' seemed at times to relieve his wife of her vacancy and despair. He continues:

> All this sounds quite merry . . . and I try to seem to explain the

> trouble. The Alzheimer face has been clinically described as the 'lion face'. An apparently odd comparison but in fact a very apt one. The Alzheimer face is neither tragic nor comic . . . [it] indicates only an absence. That is why the sudden appearance of a smile is so extraordinary . . . Only a joke survives, the last thing that finds its way into consciousness when the brain is atrophied.[4]

Right in the middle of deep pain an echo of ridiculousness lifts it. And in that moment others are included.

CONNECTIONS BETWEEN TRAGEDY AND PLAYFULNESS

Space alone will restrict the examples to two. You may like to collect others for yourself. Roly Bain expresses connection between tragedy and playfulness most potently. He writes:

> Feelings may run riot, respectability collapse, gloom and sorrow descend like nightfall, and there the clown stands in the midst of the maelstrom . . . He can dare to feel it and share it before [offering] a redeeming smile. . . . Perhaps that's the difference between clowns and comics. Clowns have that tragic dimension that comedians don't. Clowning is so important and has such mystical and mysterious connotations and connections.[5]

L'Arche is an organisation which arranges groups of houses where able-bodied men and women share their lives with those who have special needs. Among those who could not cope with living among 'ordinary' people was Nick, a man with Down's

Syndrome. Therese Vanier[6] has written of him with enormous affection and respect. She says:

> One of my most vivid memories of Nick was on a very muddy pilgrimage route to Canterbury. Nick was literally up to his knees in slush and mud, and like a child he just jumped up and down in it, threw his arms up in the air and laughed his old roguish, infectious laugh, enjoying every minute. The conditions did not do much for me, but Nick's capacity to enjoy life as it came, did a lot for me![7]

The dedication of the book is 'To the memory of Nick and to all men and women who confound our wisdom, allowing that spark of foolishness which exists in all of us to ignite and give life.'

THE FINDINGS OF SCIENCE

A different dimension to this connection between pain and the absurd is found in neurology. When we've been to a really good party with lots of fun and laughter, we sometimes find that later we feel puzzled, even guilty, that our pain had gone missing. The Creator, in his ingenuity, placed the mechanisms which produce laughter and pain very close to each other in the brain. This means there is a constant interplay which goes on between their specific neurotransmitters, and when we get 'taken out of ourselves' by laughter or enjoyment we feel pain less. The study of this phenomenon is on the frontiers of neuro-immunology. The discovered connections found have sound practical implications: they concern neurological reactions that are automatic, but they are also about skills that can be learned consciously. Either way we are supplied with a reliable coping mechanism. It is not simply a blind, or defence, or cover-up; it is a real and profound confluence or running-together of different responses to stimuli. This means that something that is a common experience in crisis (for instance: joking with a patient until the ambulance arrives) can be applied, quite deliberately, to other situations of hurting. Maybe it is something that has to be consciously learned, but then used as unselfconsciously as possible.

Our physical make-up is only the basis of what we feel emotionally. For instance:

FEELING AWFUL *AND* PLAYING?

In our anguish, for ourselves or for others, we long for a type of relief that is obvious and positive and overwhelming; what we discover is that comfort often comes in the shape of hints and whispers, rustlings and even chucklings. It is about a subtle, ingenuous and sometimes incongruous exchange. The awfulness that others are going through can indeed fill us with awe, but that in itself distances us from being alongside them. It can reinforce the 'crossing the road' syndrome. Coming along this less definable way, sometimes we can approach the hurt and the hurter a bit more positively even though we fumble at it. There are five angles to note:

(i) When I'm feeling awful, a mere touch of playfulness may prevent me from 'awfulizing' what is already bad enough. A close friend described it recently: 'When things get that bad, the only resort you've got is laughter.' The word she used is interesting: it's not about a holiday resort, but it hints at a new sorting out of priorities, a *re-sort*.

(ii) When I am feeling awful, the sharing of laughter or play or empathy may open up something which has previously been closed tight. A hug, a stroke, a giggle can begin to prise apart the prison bars which have been holding back all sorts of negativities. Perhaps at that stage they can be met by a good chortle *with* them, though never *at* them. Crying with people when they want to cry is natural and empathetic; on occasion, an alongside chuckle brings relief of a different quality.

(iii) Children are particularly good at showing the way this is done. Staff who work in hospitals or hospices have at their fingertips scores of stories about sick children and playfulness. Most of them retain the zig-zag path between pain and playfulness right up to the final stages of their illness. Jane Grayshon writes particularly sensitively about paining children.[8] She quotes one child putting it like this: 'Pain is a feeling just like gladness but pain is much sadder than gladness'; and another who says: 'If people didn't have pain that would mean a big feeling was missing; even though it would be good to be happy all the time it wouldn't be right.'

(iv) Many elderly people manage to hang on to a similar twinkle in their eyes, even though they are chronically disabled. A twinkle that redeems us all, the paining one and those alongside them: it closes the gap, and it wipes out anything akin to resentment or self-pity. There are those who have progressive or terminal illness and who describe their super-awareness of the play and enjoyment in life. An Australian poet named Marion McCall is such a one. She writes:

> Where is the Christ?
> Lying in the tomb
> With me
> Battered body, bloodied limbs
> Broken.

But later:

I feel like
Riding a motor bike
Wind tearing at my cheeks
Like on a roller-coaster ride
Screaming uphill and down again
Like the first take off
Airborne and flying
Earth far below.
Like dancing and jumping and shouting
Lifting my face to the sky.
Like all that.

I am completely overcome
By your goodness to me
I cannot speak.[9]

To cap the evidence of this difficult terrain, there is a remarkable woman from Rwanda. She saw her husband, sons, parents and siblings tortured and killed. 'I have been condemned to live,' she said, in a matter-of-fact sort of way, 'but I'm going to make sure that I am *alive-alive, not alive-dead*.'

JESUS AND 'OPTIMISM'

What about the attitude of Jesus? Jack Dominian, the renowned psychiatrist, has tried to analyse the roots of Jesus' attitudes in his life on earth. He says that while Jesus had

> the capacity to feel the inner world of others, [he still] showed optimism in his approach to disease, which he felt could be conquered, and to his own suffering, which he was convinced

would not overwhelm him. Ultimately, he was also optimistic in his awareness that death is not the end.[10]

This 'capacity to feel the inner world' means being aware of need in myself as well as in the other, then owning it, whether it is in me or in another, instead of hiding from it or disguising it. It is allowing authenticity and absurdity to hold hands over it. It is about the hurt child in Jesus coming out running to meet the hurt child in me with arms wide open.

JESUS AND HIS NEEDS

This is something to stop us in our tracks with wonder . . . It is almost thinking the unthinkable. The Gospels show that Jesus, in the full likeness of God, opened up to us *his own need*. There are times when this is the way God himself engages us. (Can we bear that prospect and still stay mentally stable?) Here are some instances:

- Jesus Christ, even as the face of God, told his disciples of his need for rest in their company.
- Many times he told those who were in pain he needed to know what they wanted of him.
- He told those around him he wanted the children near him.
- He engaged the woman at the well in Samaria by telling her of his thirst.
- He engaged the men who had tortured him, scoffed at him, driven nails into his hands and feet – by telling them, too, of his thirst.

Jesus, although he was the Son of God, was a real, pulsating, needing, human being. God makes it easier for us to tell him of our needs, by letting us know of his.

God asks us to join him in his need; he even asks some rare people to be alongside him in his incalculable grief. John Taylor puts it like this:

> It is God as Self-Giver who expresses himself continuously in the spontaneous, uncompelled outflow of love for his people. His is the pure will, that at whatever cost to himself, they should be there, and a pure delight in their being there whatever the outcome. Because this God fulfils his divinity in inexhaustible self-giving, his delight is the fierce joy of the artist or the mountaineer that persists unabated by any amount of real pain, anger or defeat. His is the bliss that can include and outshine all suffering.[11]

God, in his outpouring love, feels the pain of the world as we do but multiplied incalculably. And yet his delight in the world must be greater. As John Taylor again has pointed out, *the delight has to be greater than the pain or he would annihilate the world.*

BEING PIERCED, BUT STILL BEING WELCOMING

This is one of the deepest mysteries, that the sword and the welcome fit together. It is to do with the concept that the present piercing experience is somehow bound up into one with the invitation to play with God. If it is possible for me to be available to playfulness, even while I am hurting or disadvantaged or 'challenged' or feeling less-of-myself-than-I-could-be, then something transforming and miraculous happens.

- Did you see the TV pictures of the first train of battered refugees arriving in Albania from Kosovo? The first thing the children did as they spilled from the carriages was – to play ring-a-ring-a-roses.
- Then there is a picture of a small child, born with no bones in his lower limbs, playing with a football a few days after he was fitted with two wooden artificial legs: his arms are up in the air and he is shouting, 'I love my legs hundreds and hundreds and hundreds!' The photo is reproduced on p. 96.
- Again, a middle-aged woman I know cannot stand on her own because her spine is crumbling; it gives her excruciating pain, so she sits on the floor to play when she meets with her class of damaged people.

Maybe this is the heart of Christlikeness; maybe it is this that makes Christ-centredness unique among the great world religions. We believe that God asks us to hold the invitation and the welcome at one with the sword. It is a first priority to relieve pain and suffering, but at the core where it cannot be removed, Jesus the Christ modelled a way of extending love and play to all who would listen. In his own life he acted out the claim that the 'good cheer' he repeatedly offers us, is greater than the pain. He did so to convince us that, whatever may happen, 'all shall be well, and all shall be well, and all manner of thing shall be well'.[12]

PERSONAL REFLECTION

This amazing grace of holding pain and hurting and still being sufficiently open to welcome playfulness cannot be contrived, it can only be prayed for. It cannot be forced, but it can be received.

It is something much more than what is rather vaguely called 'a sense of humour'. When it's there, it is a gift direct from God.[13]

May the cross of Christ be over this face and this ear
May the cross of Christ be over this mouth and this throat
May the cross of Christ be over these my arms
From my shoulders to my hands.

May the cross of Christ be within me, before me;
May the cross of Christ be above me, behind me.

With the cross of Christ I meet
Every difficulty in the heights and in the depths.
From the top of my head to the nail of my toes –
I trust in your cross, O Christ.[14]

11

THE THIRD MILLENNIUM: A RE-AWAKENING OF PLAYFULNESS AND PRAYER?

The sword and the welcome are bound in one.[1]

God's values are topsy-turvy: first coming last, last coming first. Losing life and gaining it, gaining life and losing it. Adults becoming childlike, children becoming icons of the Kingdom. Hide and seek – now you see it and now you don't. Planets charging at each other in the cosmos, molecules predicting genetic inheritance. Of course the universal design is one of playfulness!

The welcoming arms and the piercing sword are bound together in a sacred paradox.

You may remember an experience of looking at a stunning picture, or listening to powerful music, or gazing at a wonderful sunset, and being unable to decide whether what moved you was joy or grief or serenity. Sometimes it's difficult to know whether such poignant moments hurt or please. The oneness of the welcome and the sword is something like that. The outstretched welcome balances the sword upright, while the long sword steadies the wide welcome. Invitation and exposure to hurt are different dimensions of the same situation; it takes a childlike quality to accept both together. Jesus said to Thomas, who was doubting the reality of his presence, 'Put your fingers into the holes in my hands and feet and side' – surely only a child would dare to finger such wounds, and only an abandoned generosity could invite such fingering.

Maybe the new century offers us a return to the valuing of child-likeness. Jesus also said: *'Watch out that you don't treat a single one of the childlike believers arrogantly. Their personal angels are constantly in touch with my Father in heaven'* (Matt. 18:10[2]).

And put more studiously a modern theologian has commented: 'Each individual each moment makes his or her own response to the environment in which she or he is situated. God delights in what evolves through the play of free creativity in the processes of reality.'[3]

THE TIMES AHEAD

Unpredictability and uncertainty are said to be the marks of the life ahead of us. Social orders, nationhoods, cultures, jobs, incidence of diseases, major conflicts, and even personal relationships – all will be marked by flux and change. Some of these insecurities we have tasted already, but usually with the hope that conditions will revert to the type of stability we have come to rely on in the past two or three centuries. We now have to face the question: if, for the predictable future, chaotic values will be all we see around us, will the Kingdom of God be furthered by digging our heels in and living obstinately as if under siege? Or do we need to relearn early ways of opening and welcoming, even if it means taking risks, and thereby gain a new experience of God's lavish generosity and unending ingenuity? Can we learn to stretch easily and gladly, to gambol (and gamble) in the presence of God, abandoned to his unquenchable, unlimited, overflowing *Love*?

Christianity has often been preached as a place of sanctuary. But in the conditions of the third millennium, and the confusion which is likely to be its characteristic, maybe different functions will be asked of it. Christ is calling us to be places where we can explore our confusions safely, enfolded in a spirit of playfulness. Maybe we have to forego some of our established borders in order to become welcoming centres of playfulness, where confusion becomes creative, and those who hurt can find both solace and fullness. *(Come, Mary's child, my Friend; our fullness is in you.*[4])

A true story:

> A young boy from Rwanda came to Britain as some respite from the tragedy in his own land. He began to learn English, but as with all speakers of Kinyarwanda, he found difficulty in mouthing the difference between 'l' and 'r'. On his return, he found that the pastor of his church was now leading services in the new tongue, English. At the end of the worship he asked his mother, puzzled: 'When he says, "Let us pray", why don't we play?'

FROM EARLY TIMES

We have a heritage of powerful images from older but similarly chaotic times when God's people were unsure; they indeed supply us with grounds for playfulness.

Listen to me; pay heed; the Lord called me before I was born, he named me from my mother's womb. Shout for joy, you heavens! Earth, rejoice! Break into songs of triumph, you mountains. For the Lord has comforted his people and has had pity on them in their distress. I shall never forget you.

'Listen to me: consider the rock from which you were hewn, the quarry from which you were cut: the Lord has comforted Zion, comforted all her ruined homes, turning her wilderness into an Eden, her arid plains into a garden of the Lord. Gladness and joy will be found in her, thanksgiving and melody. Gladness and joy will come upon them, while suffering and weariness will flee away. I am he who comforts you; why then fear man who must die? Why have you forgotten the Lord your maker, who stretched out the heavens and founded the earth? Why are you in constant fear all the time? I have put my words in your mouth, and kept you covered under the shelter of my hand. I who fixed the heavens in place and established the earth say *"You are my people"*.

'Come for water, all you who are thirsty; come, buy wine and milk. You will go out with joy, and be led forth in peace. Before you mountains and hills will break into cries of joy, and all the trees in the countryside will clap their hands.

'My servants in the gladness of their hearts will shout for joy. "See! I am creating new heavens and a new earth! Rejoice and be for ever filled with delight at what I create! I shall take delight in Jerusalem and rejoice in my people."

'Rejoice with Jerusalem and exult in her, share her joy with all your heart. Her babes will be carried in her arms and dandled on her knees; as a mother comforts her son so shall I myself comfort you.'[5]

The way ahead is a jigsaw, but it is in the hands of God and he asks us to be his children, his 'playmates'. These are some of the pieces of the jigsaw:

- When he created us, God saw fit to install in each one of us a natural, right and proper urge to look out for our own wellbeing; but it is also his intention that that search includes the looking out for the wellbeing of our neighbour. It is impossible to achieve the fullness of wellbeing of either without a dependence on him for his power, presence, purpose and peace. The whole is a package, and what glues it together is Love, and the expression of love is Delight.[6]
- We know that Jesus' body (– his carapace, his shell –) died on Good Friday: but not his love. Love was hidden on Holy Saturday, when traditionally Love was harrowing hell. And Love exploded into its world again on Easter Day and it still explodes around us in minute detail and in large-scale witness, in sacrifice and in welcome and in exuberance. Continual mini-surprises dropping on us unawares like manna – or at times the exhilaration of a maxi-surprise. The evidence is everywhere, but, like playing tag, we have to search it out and acclaim it, in joy and trust and celebration. Such is the role of playfulness.
- At times we each find we are faced with evil; are we to be pressured and overloaded – or positively playful? This is the strange thing we are being invited to reconsider. Much of the previous century saw a growing conviction that to state one's feelings was just and liberating. There is a growing awareness that this is not universally applicable. Putting a present point of view into words can somehow seal it; it is there to be examined. But the next day the experience, and one's view of it, may have changed. Wild beasts can be captured and studied by scientists, or they can be simply sensed in the undergrowth, acknowledged but not challenged, and the wild beast melts back

again into own territory. Threats can sometimes be disarmed by not looking at them too closely, and that is another form of play. Maybe an easy story will illustrate this.

> Pam was dependent on her pen. When she woke each day she planned the stories she would write, the cheques she would sign, the consoling notes she would send. One morning the pen got lost: Pam was nearly distraught. Panic tugged at her throat; frustration, worry and outrage were on the tip of her tongue. She locked them behind bars for two hours while she looked for her pen, forcing the urgency to stay out of sight. It was no good.
>
> Pam sat down and deliberately thought of her beloved pen. Was it happily playing a game of hide and seek? Safe and comfortable, was it chuckling at its success at remaining hidden, and just biding its time? Pam let it be and turned to the neglected garden.
>
> Time passed and evening came. Still no sign of the pen. Bedtime arrived and Pam lay down surprised at how the activity in the garden had revitalised her. She laid her ear on the pillow and felt the bulge of the pen. It had been there all day, with neither malice nor guile. Pam chuckled; perhaps it, too, had just needed a rest.

WHAT GOD WANTS OF US

How can we put this knowledge of the sword-plus-the-welcome into practice? Trevor Hudson, who ministers in some of the most troubled parts of South Africa, expresses it like this:

> Seeking to live the compassionate life had become a grim and heavy-hearted enterprise. Indeed, I felt that enjoying

myself was a betrayal of the pain and anguish of those suffering around me. Not only did I view life through sombre and dark spectacles, but even my picture of God assumed a rather gloomy countenance. Unlike the joyful Nazarene whose footsteps I sought to follow, and who was accused of being a wine-bibber and glutton.[7]

To get through the world alive we have to care until our hearts break and cram our lives full of enjoyment. Both/and, not either/or . . . The great trinity of virtues – joy, gratitude, and care – is inseparable. Only enjoyment and gratitude for our lives create a spontaneous impulse to care for others.[8]

The more we are made aware of the evil in the world, the stronger the evidence of horror and debasement, the more imperative it is that we assert goodness, trust, play and laughter. We have a huge opportunity not just to make use of these things for our own personal coping skills, but to enlarge their presence in the world.

God requires ammunition from us for him to use against the Opposer. There are two sorts we can hand to him. Firstly it is our suffering, and what we do with it. What *can* we do with it? I was asked recently: was I willing to let God *use* my pain? Or was I going to let it get dissipated and to waste the power of it? Ultimately, am I prepared to be alongside God in the grief he carries for the waywardness of his creation?

The other sort of ammunition we can offer to God in the cosmic fight against evil is our acknowledgement and acceptance of his joy and delight in his world. The many and multiple gifts which we receive from him every day. Our delight in the knowledge that they belong to God, and are of God. They are not ours to clutch at and possess. They are offered to us to enjoy and then give them back; we are accountable for the way in which we receive and handle every boon, every grace, whether it is intangible or concrete. And whether we play with it in wonder, or whether we possess it, greedily.

At all times, we can allow God's sense of humour to get in the way of us becoming too pompous, too self-important, too solemn.

IN SUMMARY

Charles Péguy is a remarkable French poet, who died in the trenches in 1914. His radical views were presented in long poems spoken as if by God. In these lines selected from 'The Holy Innocents' he creates a synopsis of much of this book:

God says:

My Son had been a tender, milky child;
a childhood, a burgeoning, a promise, an engagement;
an attempt; an origin; a beginning of a Redeemer;
a hope of salvation; a hope of redemption. . . .

Faith is a great tree, an oak rooted in the heart;
and under the wings of that tree Charity, my daughter,
shelters all the distress of the world.
And my little hope is only that little promise of a bud which
shows itself at the very beginning of April.
And I tell you, God says, without those thousands, without that
little burgeoning of hope, which obviously everybody can
break, without that tender downy bud, which the first comer
can nip off with his nail, all my creation would be nothing
but dead wood. . . .

I know man well. It is I who made him. He is a strange creature.

For in him operates that liberty which is the mystery of mysteries.
Still one can ask a great deal from him. He is not too bad. You must not say he is bad.
He has plenty of faith and plenty of charity.
But what one can't ask of him, damn it, is a little hope.
A little confidence, what, a little relaxation.
A little delay, a little abandonment.
That is the one who pleases me, says God.
The one who rests in my arms like a laughing baby.
The man who abandons himself, I love.
I have often played with man, God says. But what a game! It is a game that makes me tremble.
I have often played with man, but, by God, it was in order to save him, and I have trembled enough because I might not be able to save him;
Asking myself if I should succeed in saving him.[9]

The attraction and the virtue of playfulness is quite specific. It is the invitation and the welcome 'Come on in: come and join us'. To quote Roly Bain again: 'You can't force people to love nor can you make them come out to play; but you can keep on inviting and tempting and teasing' them to do so.[10]

It is an unsung, inarticulated longing that underlies everything recorded about Jesus' way of welcome. It first finds a home in the child. The child that is open to the invitation of the tree to climb up higher, but knows also of the risk. This inherent childlikeness is what Jesus tells us he most values. What has happened to yours and mine? Stop filtering: open your arms wide and welcome. Welcome the child in you, and let that child welcome the child in others. Most of all, be aware that we are *all* welcomed by the child in Jesus.

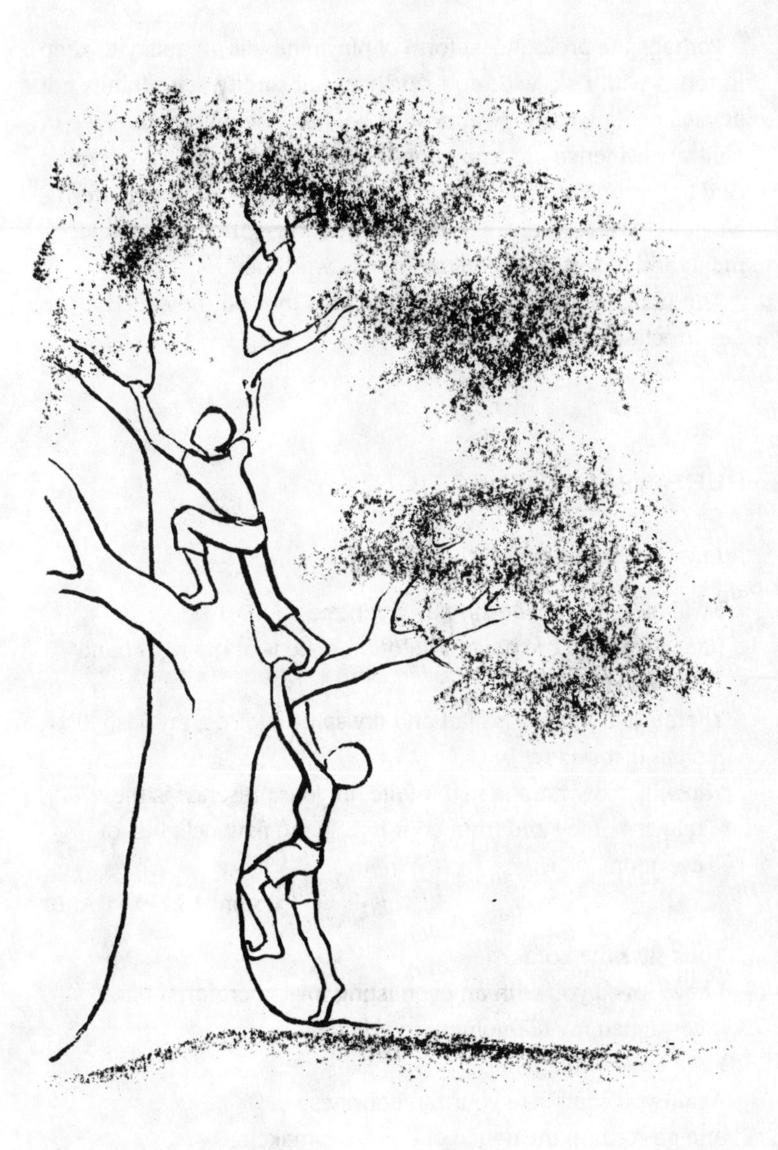

Perhaps the profoundest form of playfulness is an ability to keep in touch with risk, with non-sense and absurdity, with things not always being what they appear to be: hanging on – in the face of contrary evidence – to a firm confidence in God's purposes. Inviting God to throw it all up in the air so it falls back in another pattern – his pattern. It requires openness and courage, trust and abandonment, and a deep faith that the risk is worth it.

The ultimate goal has been shown us by God: he called it the Resurrection.

PERSONAL REFLECTION

A few verses with which to conclude:

I will bless the Lord who has given me counsel . . .
I have set the Lord always before me: he is at my right hand
and I shall not fall.
Therefore my heart is glad and my spirit rejoices; my flesh also
shall rest secure . . .
You will show me the path of life: in your presence is the
fullness of joy and from your right hand flow delights for
evermore.

(Psalm 16:7–9,11 ASB)

Thus says the Lord:
I have loved you with an everlasting love, therefore I have
continued my faithfulness to you . . .
I will build you again . . .
Again you shall take your tambourines,
and go forth in the dance of the merrymakers.

(Jeremiah 31:2–4 ASB)

Lord, take all our longings and aspirations, our yearnings and frustrations at our own inadequacy, our intentions and failings; our eagerness and our obstinacy. Accept and absorb them into your power and purpose; make them part of your great juggling act, and mould them into your plan of transforming the world to your glory. For I know that your desire is to smile the world back into new life.[11] *You don't need to tell me, Lord, what you would laughingly do with trembling me for your incredible world; I simply ask that you do it.*[12]

There comes a moment when it is not simply a matter of invitation and welcome: God's presence is there before I am. The Presence of God is inviting me and welcoming me a hundredfold more warmly than I could ever imagine. And the exchange is of such inequality that it is absurd. The notion that I can offer myself to God to the extent that God offers himself to me is so patently ridiculous that I have to burst out laughing. I am struck dumb by the playfulness of the suggestion that I am in him as he is in me. But it is such playfulness that I cannot refuse, and I leap into his arms to be enfolded and held. And playful as he is, God catches me and hugs me. And you . . . and you . . . and you . . . and you . . .

And so, fall down and adore – and then come, let us play.

NOTES

Epigraph

1. Matthew Fox, *Original Blessing* (Santa Fe: Bear & Co., 1983), p. 222.

***Chapter 1:* WHY NOW? WHY TODAY?**

1. Gerard Hughes SJ, *God, Where Are You?* (London: Darton, Longman & Todd, 1977), p. 28.
2. *Dictionary of Word Origins*, ed. John Ayto (Columbia Marketing, 1990). ISBN 185980 0076.
3. Neh. 8:9–17 AV (contracted).
4. From Dorothy Sayers, *Unpopular Opinions* (London: Victor Gollancz, 1946), p. 9.
5. Roly Bain, *Fools Rush In – a Call to Christian Clowning* (London: Marshall Pickering, 1993), p. 39. ISBN 0–551–02733–9.
6. This headline was featured on 21 February 1999.
7. Robert Holden has been popular on TV, and written several books on the subject of instant happiness. They include *Laughter – the Best Medicine, Living Wonderfully* and *Happiness Now!* This last was published by Hodder & Stoughton in 1998.
8. Contact address: The Julian Meetings, 9 Milward Close, Haverford West, Dyfed, SA61 2SS.
9. Contact address: The World Community for Christian Meditation, 23 Kensington Square, London, W8 5HN.
10. By Ann Lewin, who has kindly consented to the inclusion of this poem here. It is selected from her book *Candles and Kingfishers*, 1993.

***Chapter 2:* CHILDISHNESS AND CHILDLIKENESS**

1. The antecedent 'com' denotes an attitude of fellow-feeling, of being together, in combination or union; it is about something that is marked by strong emotion, as in 'comfort', or 'company', 'accompany', and 'companion'.
2. This characterisation is brilliantly illustrated in the book *Jesus' Day-Off* by Nicholas Allan (London: Hutchinson's, 1998). ISBN 0–09–176749–0. Although it is prepared as a children's book, it should be read by every ordained person and their advisers everywhere!

3. See the author's *Gifts from Hildegard* (London: Darton Longman & Todd Ltd, 1997).
4. See also Matt. 18:2; Mark 9:36f. and 10:15; Luke 18:17.
5. See *Prayers from the Ark*, by Carmen Bernos de Gasztold, translated by Rumer Godden (Macmillan 1963 and reprinted until 1971). ISBN 333–05586–1.

***Chapter 3:* JESUS AND THE CHILDREN**

1. Other versions include: 'and the child . . . waxed strong in spirit, and the grace of God was upon him' (AV); 'grew big and strong and full of wisdom, and God's favour was upon him' (REB); and 'there the child grew strong in body and wise in spirit. And the grace of God was on him' (*The Message*).
2. Tom Wright, Dean, suggests that even at the last supper, when Jesus was confronting the tortured ending to his earthly life and offering his last instructions to his disciples, he used the strategy of 'teasing' when he answered their puzzlement by saying, 'You already know the way'. See his book *Reflecting the Glory* (London: Bible Reading Fellowship, 1997), p. 128.
3. 'If anyone causes the downfall of one of these little ones who believe in me, it would be better for him to have a millstone hung round his neck and be drowned in the depths of the sea. Alas for the world that any of them should be made to fall!' Matt. 18:6–7 (REB). Also Mark 9:42; Luke 17:2.
4. Writer and psychiatrist. One of his books explores this subject in detail. See *One Like Us* (London: Darton, Longman & Todd Ltd, 1998).
5. Mark 9:36; 10:16.
6. Luke 23:28. See also Luke 19:44; 21:23; Matt. 24:19; Mark 13:17 – expressing pity for children and mothers during the terrors ahead.
7. Matt. 11:19; Luke 7:35.
8. Luke 18:15–17, see also Matt. 19:13; Mark 10:13, in addition to references already cited which include instances where Jesus proactively called children to him – Matt. 18:2; Mark 9:36; 10:15; Luke 9:47; 18:17.
9. See Matt. 18:6; 18:10,14; Mark 9:42; Luke 17:2.
10. Matt. 18:10,14.
11. Matt. 21:15 – the children shouting 'Hosanna to the Son of David' in the temple; and Matt. 21:16 – Jesus quoting Psalm 8:2 to the disapproving Pharisees: 'By the mouths of children, babes in arms, you have made sure of praise'.
12. Matt. 10:21, Mark 13:12 are in the form of warnings of what may happen; Matt. 19:29, Mark 10:29–30, and Luke 14:26, 18:29–30 are all acknowledging that loyalty to Christ may bring out divisions within families; perhaps most poignant of all, Jesus' experience of the need to separate from his own mother is expressed in Luke 2:48 and Matt. 12:48 and Mark 3:33.
13. See Matt. 11:16; Luke 7:32.
14. John 6:9.
15. Matt. 15:22–8; Mark 7:25–30.

16. Matt. 17:14–18; Mark 9:14–27; Luke 9:37–42.
17. Matt. 9:18–19, 23–6; Mark 5:22–4, 35–43; Luke 8:41–2, 49–56.
18. John 4:46–53.
19. For instance, Luke 20:36: Jesus says, 'They are like angels; they are the children of God, because they share in the resurrection' (REB). John 1:12: 'to all who did accept him he gave power to become children of God' (JB).
    John 11:52: 'Jesus was to die... to gather together in unity the scattered children of God' (JB).
20. See Matt. 11:25: 'I bless you, Father, . . . for . . . revealing these things to little children' (NJB); see also Luke 10:21.
    Mark 10:24: 'The disciples were astounded, but Jesus insisted, "My children . . . how hard it is to enter the kingdom of God"' (NJB).
    John 13:33: 'Little children, I shall not be with you much longer' (NJB).
    John 21:5: 'Have you caught anything, my children?' (JB)
21. Matt. 23:37; Luke 13:34,35.
22. Peter Byrne CSSR, from *The Laughter of Christ*, a small privately printed booklet produced by Redemptorist Monastery, Ireland, in 1989.

Chapter 4: PLAY, LAUGHTER, AND WONDER: SOME OF THE FACTS

1. See 2 Sam. 6:21–2. Also 2 Sam. 6:5 and 1 Sam.19:24.
2. Rebecca Abrams, *The Playful Self* (London: Fourth Estate, 1997), p. 31.
3. Aric Sigman, *New, Improved?* (London: Simon and Schuster, 1995).
4. ibid, p. 178.
5. See also Karl-Joseph Kuschel, *Laughter: A Theological Reflection* (London: SCM Press, 1994).
6. This entire subject of laughter has been expanded more fully by the author in *Christ, Stress and Glory*, chapter 18, and in *Turning the Downside Up*, chapter 2. For further details see Booklist.
7. Henri Nouwen, *Sabbatical Journey: The Diary of his Final Year* (London: Darton, Longman and Todd Ltd, 1998), pp. 5–6, my italics.
8. Tom Wright, *Reflecting the Glory* (London: Bible Reading Fellowship, 1997).

Chapter 5: WHY SHOULD ADULTS *WANT* TO PLAY?

1. Therapist and trainer, editor of *The Therapist*, and director of the European Therapy Studies Institute.
2. Michael Sky, *Sexual Peace* (Santa Fe: Bear & Co., 1951), p. 118.
3. Marion Milner, born 1900, author of such influential books as *A Life of One's Own, 1934; Experiment With Leisure*; and *The Hands of the Living God*. The above piece is derived from an article in *The Observer*, Feb. 1987.
4. Carl G. Jung, as quoted in Matthew Fox, *Original Blessing* (Santa Fe: Bear & Co., 1983), p. 138.

5. David Pailin, *Gentle Touch: from a theology of handicap to a theology of human being* (London: SPCK, 1992).
6. See Matthew Fox, *Original Blessing*, p. 222.
7. This extraordinary quality is looked at in greater depth in chapter 9 'Playing Among the Mystics'.
8. Extracted from an article by Gayle Privette, 'Peak Experience, Peak Performance, and Flow: a Comparative Analysis of Positive Human Experiences' in *Personality and Social Psychology* 1983, vol. 45, no. 6, 1361–8, in which she refers to the work of Laski, Maslow, Privette, Huizinga, and Csikszentmihalyi during the period of 1962–83.
9. Wayne Sotile, *Psychosocial Interventions: a Guide for Health Professsionals* (Leeds: Human Kinetics, 1996).
10. Devised by Anthony de Mello, and described in his biography *Unencumbered by Baggage* (published by Gujarat Sahitya Prakash, India).

***Chapter 6:* DID JESUS LAUGH AND PLAY?**

1. See also Exod. 17:6; Neh. 9:15; Ps. 114:8; Isa. 43:20; Ezek. 47:1,9; Zech. 14:8; Rev. 22:1,2.
2. Matt. 3:17 (cited from Isa. 42); see also Matt. 12:18–20; Mark 9:7; Luke 9:35, the voice of God at the Transfiguration; John 12:27ff., Jesus' answer to the enquiring Greeks as he was about to enter his passion: ' "Now is my soul troubled; and what shall I say? . . . Father, glorify thy name." Then came there a voice from heaven, saying, "I have both glorified it, and will glorify it again"' (AV).
3. Admittedly, this is partly due to the difficulty of capturing a passing moment in a permanent form. Several American artists were asked to paint Christ laughing, with varying success. The book is now out of print.
4. There are at least 40 references in the Gospels to Jesus deliberately withdrawing from the public eye; of them, nine are to withdraw in order to 'rest with his disciples'. See the author's *Christ, Stress and Glory*, ch.11.
5. Whether this is a reference to a narrow gate named 'the eye of a needle' or is intended to reflect a familiar domestic difficulty, the incongruity remains.
6. Matt. 15:27 and Mark 7:28, from *The Message* by Eugene Peterson (1993). See also the GNB version: 'The woman came and fell at his feet, "Help me, sir!" she said. Jesus answered, "It isn't right to take the children's food and throw it to the dogs." "That's true, sir," she answered, "but even the dogs eat the leftovers that fall from their master's table." So Jesus answered her, "You are a woman of great faith! What you want will be done for you." And at that very moment her daughter was healed.'
7. For other examples where 'O ye of little faith' is used in answer to a situation of anxiety and despair, see Matt. 8:26; Mark 4:40; Luke 8:25 (stilling of the storm); and Matt. 6:30; Luke 12:28 (concerning anxiety over material needs).
8. Also Matt. 26:33–5; Mark 14:29–33; Luke 22:33–4.

9. It is sometimes tempting to use another of Carroll's verbal inventions. Did Jesus know about *galumphing* – to bound exultingly, in a sort of triumphant gallop? I can well imagine the children doing just this all round about him.
10. Of course, there were other times when Jesus' rebuke was severe. For instance, see Matt. 16:8.
11. The 'windbag' of the medieval fool was made out of a pig's *belly!*
12. Tom Wright, academician, writer, theological communicator, writes of Jesus' use of 'teasing' as a method for making his point even in the course of the Last Supper. He describes Jesus' remark, 'You know the way to the place where I am going' as teasing, and his response to Philip, 'Have I been with you all this time, and you still do not know me?' as a 'teasing' question (John 14:4,9). See *Reflecting the Glory* (Oxford: BRF, 1997), pp. 128, 131.

***Chapter 7:* GOD AND PLAYFULNESS**

1. John Taylor, *The Christlike God* (London: SCM Press Ltd, 1992).
2. As the father of the home-coming prodigal son *ran* towards him, arms outstretched. Did you know that God has placed in the knees of fleas and the elbows of dragonflies – uniquely and specifically – a protein of such power that if it were inserted into a man's knees he could jump up to the top of London's GPO tower 22,000 times without tiring?
3. Michael Mayne, *Pray, Love, Remember* (London: Darton, Longman & Todd Ltd, 1999).
4. Tom Wright, *Reflecting the Glory* (Oxford: BRF, 1997), p. 89.
5. And in the *ruach* of the Holy Spirit: 'The wind blows wherever it wishes; you hear the sound it makes, but you do not know where it comes from or where it is going' (John 3:8 GNB).

***Chapter 8:* PLAYFULNESS IN *ME*?**

1. Some versions go 'Come with a hoop and come with a ball'.
2. Helen Caswell, *God Must Like to Laugh* (Cambridge: Lutterworth Press, 1987).
3. Richard Holloway, *Dancing on the Edge* (London: HarperCollins Religious, 1997).
4. Harry Williams, *Tensions* (London: Michael Beazley Publishers, 1976), p. 111.
5. It is important to distinguish this sort of passing mood depression, however real and genuine it is, from that which is pathological and needs professional help.
6. See 1 Cor. 4:10.
7. Ordained in 1978, Roly Bain went to circus school 1990–1 and was chosen as 'Clown of the Year' in 1994.
8. Roly Bain, *Fools Rush In – a Call to Christian Clowning* (London: Marshall Pickering, 1993), p. 80.
9. As note 8 above.
10. Derived from information heard on BBC4. The programme included the state-

ment: 'Of course, this new discovery is a mere forty-four light years away, it is positively on our doorstep'!

11. See John 15:13–15 (also Luke 12:14). Some translators have used the word 'guest' in this context.

***Chapter 9:* PLAYING AMONG THE MYSTICS**

1. A Celtic prayer, very powerful as a 'mantra'.
2. See Edith Scholl, *To Be a Bride: Mechthild of Magdeburg* (1209–1283 AD), pp. 223–38, in Nichols and Shank (eds.), *Peace Weavers* Vol. II (Michigan: Cistercian Publications Inc., 1987).
3. Quote from Meister Eckhart (thirteenth century). Printed on a poster.
4. I am grateful to Prof. Brian Mahoney at Hull University for citing this incident.
5. See Christopher Coelho, *A New Kind of Fool*. ISBN 0–86012–184–4.
6. From *The Revelations of Divine Love* (1373 AD), ed. Dom Hudleston (London: Burns & Oates, 1952). Extracts from chs. 14, 23, and 10, 40, 73, 88, 81.
7. Quotations taken from *The Cloud of Unknowing* (*1393* AD) as translated by Robert Way (Anthony Clarke, 1986, reprinted 1994). In order of quotation these selections are: ch. 4, p. 16; ch. 48, p. 74; ch. 46, p. 72; ch. 45 pp. 70–1; ch. 53, p. 81; ch. 34, p. 57; ch. 74, p. 96.
8. ibid., *Letter of Private Direction*, pp. 115, 117, 145.
9. Francois de Sales (1567–1622), *The Spiritual Conferences, Book 111*. Letter to Mme de Chantal, a widow. This St Francis is the patron saint of authors!
10. Thomas Traherne (1637–74), *Centuries: a hand book to Felicity* (London: Mowbrays, 1960). ISBN 0–264–67066–3.
11. From the introduction by Hilda Vaughan; a book that encourages us to 'behold the world no longer besmirched, but how its Creator made it: all radiant for our delight.'
12. ibid, sections 15, 17, 16, 21, 89.
13. St John Chrysostum, *c.* 347–407, preacher of Antioch and Constantinople, is well recognised as one of the greatest of Christian expositors.
14. *Everything As Divine: The Wisdom of Meister Eckhart*, translated by Colledge and McGinn (NJ: Paulist Press, 1996), p. 63, Counsel 17. ISBN 0–8091–3675–9.

***Chapter 10:* ALONGSIDE THE PAIN AND THE HURT**

1. Henry Suso (1295–1366), *The Little Book of Eternal Wisdom*, ch. xiv. Quoted in *A Dazzling Darkness*, ed. Patrick Grant (London: Fount Paperbacks, 1985), p. 221. A pupil of Meister Eckhart, Henry Suso was admired by Thomas à Kempis. His written spiritual counsel is shot through with humour and playfulness.
2. 'Inspired' by A.A. Milne (London: Methuen, 1996). ISBN 0–416–19375–7.
3. See particularly the place of humour as an antidote to despair and degradation in Brian Keenan, *An Evil Cradling* (London: Vintage, 1992). ISBN 0–09–999030–X.
4. John Bayley, *Iris* (London: Duckworth, 1998), pp. 44–5. ISBN 0–7156–2848–8.

5. Roly Bain, *Fools Rush In* (London: Marshall Pickering, 1993), p. 153.
6. Therese is the sister of Jean Vanier, the founder of the L'Arche communities.
7. Therese Vanier, *Nick: Man of the Heart* (Dublin: Gill and Macmillan, 1993), p. 19. ISBN 07171-2080-5.
8. Jane Grayshon, *In Times of Pain* (Oxford: Lion Publishing). ISBN 0-7459-1827-1.
9. Marion McCall, *Dreaming in Willochra* (South Australia: Seaview Press, 1998). ISBN 1-876070-77-3.
10. Jack Dominian, *One Like Us* (London: Darton, Longman & Todd, 1998), p. 66.
11. John Taylor, *The Christlike God*, 175. He continues: 'We would do well to recognise more gladly that God's In-Othered Self, the Spirit, searching their inmost being, and pleading through their inarticulate groans, not only affirmed their spirits that they and all God's people were still God's children, but it explored for them even the depth of God's own nature.'
12. The claim of Dame Julian of Norwich, repeated in several passages all through her *Revelations of Divine Love*. See the Booklist.
13. This is very personal, but other people will talk of very similar experience. It happens only in the depths of stillness. At some rare and unforgettable times, when wrestling with a real distress, a deep gurgling rumble is felt at the centre of the body. It is in the place where still prayer is most centred. It erupts with a total conviction in the trustworthiness of God, and it bursts up and out in a freeing, unbinding laughter that explodes the bonds of despair. Its roots are the love and God and his incomprehensible ability to turn all things around for good. In Karl Rahner's words, it is something of the sheer audacity, and is evidence of the incongruous ingenuity, of the Holy Spirit. The Triune God has everything in his hands, *everything is in hand*. The Celtic invitation 'Come, Mary's Son, my Friend, our fullness is in You' is the consequent outburst. I am left convinced I need to *invite* God every more profoundly into my life.
14. Attributed to Mugron, Abbot of Iona from 965 AD, quoted in *Celtic Daily Light*, compiled by Ray Simpson (London: Hodder & Stoughton, 1997). ISBN 0-340-69488.

***Chapter 11:* THE THIRD MILLENNIUM: A RE-AWAKENING OF PLAYFULNESS AND PRAYER?**

1. Reflecting Simeon's acclamation to God on seeing the infant Jesus and his mother: 'for mine eyes have seen thy salvation . . . a light to lighten . . . for the glory of thy people . . . that the inner thoughts of many shall be revealed – and a sword shall pierce through your own soul' (Luke 2:28–35 NRSV).
2. Taken from *The Message;* REB puts it: 'See that you do not despise one of these little ones. I tell you, they have their angels in heaven, who look continually on the face of my heavenly Father.'
3. David Pailin, *A Gentle Touch: from a theology on handicap to a theology of human being* (London: SPCK, 1992).

4. This line, mentioned at the beginning and in the personal reflection of chapter 9, is derived from an ancient Celtic rune and is used as a profound prayer-mantra.
5. Isaiah 49:1, 13, 15; 51:1, 3, 11, 12, 13, 16; 55:1, 12; 65:14, 17, 18, 19; 66:10, 12, 13 (REB).
6. See, for instance, John Piper's insistence on 'Christian hedonism' in his book *Desiring God* (Leicester: Inter-Varsity Press, 1989 reprinted 1998).
7. Trevor Hudson, *Compassionate Caring* (Guildford: Eagle, 1999), p. 89.
8. Sam Keen, *Fire in the Belly* (London: Piatkus, 1992), p. 171.
9. Charles Péguy, *The Holy Innocents and other poems*, tr. Pansy Pakenham (London: Harvill Press, 1956). Selected lines from pp. 71–97.
10. Roly Bain, *Fools Rush In – a Call to Christian Clowning* (London: Marshall Pickering, 1993), p. 151.
11. This last telling phrase is from Tom Wright's *Reflecting the Glory*. See Booklist.
12. The end of a prayer quoted by Donald Coggan in his *The Servant Son*. See Booklist.

BOOKLIST

Abrams, Rebecca, *The Playful Self* (London: Fourth Estate, 1997).

Allan, Nicholas, *Jesus' Day Off* (London: Hutchinson, 1998).

Bain, Roly, *Fools Rush In – a Call to Christian Clowning* (London: Marshall Pickering, 1993).

Blue, Lionel and Magonet, Jonathan, *How to Get Up When Life Gets You Down* (London: HarperCollins, 1992).

Caswell, Helen, *God Must Like to Laugh* (Cambridge: Lutterworth Press, 1987).

Cloud of Unknowing, tr. Robert Way (Wheathampstead: Anthony Clarke, 1994).

Coelho, Christopher, OSM, *A New Kind of Fool* (London: Burns & Oates, 1991).

Coggan, Donald, *The Servant Son* (London: SPCK, 1997).

Cotter, Jim, *Love Re-kindled – practising hospitality* (Sheffield: Cairns Publications, 1996).

Cousins, Norman, *Anatomy of an Illness* (New York: E.P. Dutton, 1976).

– *Head First – The Biology of Hope* (New York: E.P. Dutton, 1989), ch. 10 'The Laughter Connection'.

Dicken, Helene, *Full Face to God* (London: SPCK, 1971).

Dominian, Jack, *One Like Us* (London: Darton, Longman & Todd, 1998).

Eckhart, Meister, *Everything As Divine: The Wisdom of Meister Eckhart*, tr. Colledge and McGinn (NJ: Paulist Press, 1996).

Fox, Matthew, *Original Blessing* (Santa Fe: Bear & Co., 1983).

de Gasztold, Carmen Bernos, *Prayers from the Ark*, tr. Rumer Godden (London, Macmillan, 1963).

Grey, Mary, *The Wisdom of Fools*? (London: SPCK, 1993).

Hamel Cooke, Christopher, *A Time to Laugh* (London: Arthur James, 1993).

Hodgkinson, Liz, *Smile Therapy* (London: Macdonald & Co., 1987).

Holden, Robert, *Laughter, the Best Medicine* (London: Thorsons, 1993).

– *Happiness Now* (London: Hodder & Stoughton, 1999).

Holloway, Richard, *Dancing on the Edge* (London: HarperCollins, 1997).

Hudson, Trevor, *Compassionate Caring* (Guildford: Eagle, 1999), ch. 6 'Preventing Compassion Fatigue'.

Hughes, Gerard, SJ, *God, Where Are You*? (London: Darton, Longman & Todd Ltd, 1997).

Booklist

Huizinga, *Homo Ludens – a study of the play-element in culture*, tr. 1944 (London: Routledge & Kegan Paul, 1944).

Julian, Dame, *The Revelations of Divine Love* (1373 AD), ed. Dom Hudleston (London: Burns & Oates, 1952).

Keen, Sam, *Fire in the Belly* (London: Piatkus, 1992).

Kuschel, Karl-Joseph, *Laughter: A Theological Reflection* (London: SCM Press, 1994).

Lewin, Ann, *Candles and Kingfishers* (available from Methodist Publishing House, Peterborough).

Mayne, Michael, *Pray, Love, Remember* (London: Darton, Longman & Todd Ltd, 1999).

McCall, Marion, *Dreaming in Willochra* (Seaview Press, PO Box 234, Henley Beach, South Australia).

Mello, Anthony de, *Awareness* (London: Fount Paperbacks, 1990).

Nash, Wanda, *People Need Stillness* (London: Darton, Longman & Todd, 1992).

– *Turning the Downside Up* (London: HarperCollins, 1995).

– *Christ, Stress and Glory* (London: Darton, Longman & Todd, 1997).

– *Gifts from Hildegard* (London: Darton, Longman & Todd, 1997).

Nouwen, Henri, *Sabbatical Journey: The Diary of his Final Year* (London: Darton, Longman & Todd Ltd, 1998).

Pailin, David, *Gentle Touch: from a theology of handicap to a theology of human being* (London: SPCK, 1992).

Péguy, Charles, *The Holy Innocents and other poems*, tr. Pansy Pakenham (London: Harvill Press, 1956).

Peterson, Eugene, *The Message* (Colorado: Navpress, 1993).

Piper, John, *Desiring God* (Leicester: Inter-Varsity Press, 1989 reprinted 1998).

Samra, Cal, *The Joyful Christ – the Healing Power of Humour* (San Francisco: Harper, 1985).

Scholl, Edith, *To Be a Bride: Mechthild of Magdeburg* (1209–1283 AD), pp. 223–38, in Nichols and Shank (eds.), *Peace Weavers*, Vol. II (Michigan: Cistercian Publications Inc., 1987).

Sigman, Aric, *New, Improved?* (London: Simon and Schuster, 1995).

Sky, Michael, *Sexual Peace* (Santa Fe: Bear & Co., 1951), p. 118.

Sotile, Wayne, *Psychosocial Interventions: a Guide for Health Professionals* (Leeds: Human Kinetics, 1996).

Taylor, John, *The Christlike God* (London: SCM Press Ltd, 1992).

Trueblood, Charles, *The Humour of Christ* (London: Darton, Longman & Todd, 1964).

Valles, Carlos, *Unencumbered by Baggage – Tony de Mello, a prophet for our times* (Gujurat Prakash, India).

Williams, Harry, *Tensions* (London: Michael Beazley Publishers, 1976).

Wright, Tom, *Reflecting the Glory* (Oxford: BRF, 1997).